DETROIT PUBLIC LIBRARY

3 5674 00

P9-AOK-007

DETROIT PUBLIC LIBRARY

CHASE BRANCH LIBRARY
17731 W. SEVEN MILE RD.
DETROIT, MI 48235
DATE DUE

MAY 1 9 1998

ALSO BY MARTIN GILBERT

British History Atlas
Recent History Atlas: 1870 to the Present Day
The Roots of Appeasement
The European Powers
The Appeasers (*with Richard Gott*)
Winston Churchill (*Clarendon Biographies*)

Editions of documents

Britain and Germany Between the Wars
Plough My Own Furrow: the Life of Lord Allen of Hurtwood
Servant of India: Diaries of the Viceroy's Private Secretary 1905–1910
Churchill (*Spectrum Books*)
Lloyd George (*Spectrum Books*)

AMERICAN HISTORY ATLAS

AMERICAN HISTORY ATLAS

MARTIN GILBERT

Fellow of Merton College, Oxford

Cartography by ARTHUR BANKS

The Macmillan Company

911.73
G374a

C.1

OCT '69

© *1968 by Martin Gilbert*

All rights reserved. No part of this book may be reproduced or transmitted in any form or by any means, electronic or mechanical, including photocopying, recording or by any information storage and retrieval system, without permission in writing from the Publisher.

Library of Congress Catalog Card Number: 71-85777

First American Edition 1969

American History Atlas *was first published in Great Britain in 1968 by Weidenfeld and Nicolson, London*

The Macmillan Company

Printed in the United States of America

C H
Ref.

Preface

The idea for this atlas came to me while I was teaching at the
University of South Carolina. Its aim is to provide a short but
informative visual guide to American history. I have tried to make
use of maps in the widest possible way, designing each one
individually, and seeking to transform statistics and facts into
something easily seen and grasped. My material has been
obtained from a wide range of historical works, encyclopaedias
and newspaper reports. I have tried to be as comprehensive as
possible, consistent with clarity; only the reader can judge if I
have succeeded.

I should like to thank my staff colleagues and graduate
students at the University of South Carolina, who stimulated my
interest in American history. I am particularly grateful to
Professor Robert D. Ochs, head of the history faculty there, who
invited me to the University. I have been helped on the maps
themselves by many people, and should like to thank especially
Mr Preston Crews, Miss Rosemary Byrnes, Mr William Sweeney,
Mr Edmund Ranallo, Mrs Jean Kelly and Mr Tony Lawdham
for their advice and enthusiasm.

Once again I am deeply grateful to Mr Arthur Banks and his
team of cartographers, who have turned my sketches and
instructions into artwork of a high quality; and once again I
should welcome any criticism of the maps, notice of errors, and
suggestions for further maps.

MARTIN GILBERT
Merton College, Oxford

1968

List of Maps

AMERICAN HISTORY ATLAS

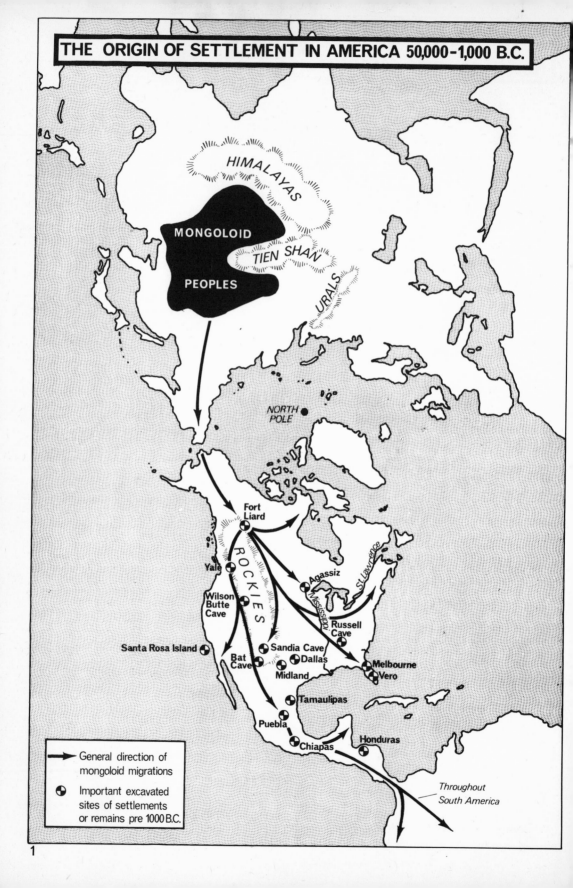

THE ORIGIN OF SETTLEMENT IN AMERICA 50,000-1,000 B.C.

HIMALAYAS

MONGOLOID

TIEN SHAN

PEOPLES

URALS

NORTH POLE

Fort Liard

ROCKIES

Yale

St. Lawrence

Agassiz

Wilson Butte Cave

Mississippi

Russell Cave

Santa Rosa Island

Sandia Cave

Dallas

Bat Cave

Midland

Melbourne
Vero

Tamaulipas

Puebla

Chiapas

Honduras

Throughout South America

→ General direction of mongoloid migrations

⊕ Important excavated sites of settlements or remains pre 1000 B.C.

1

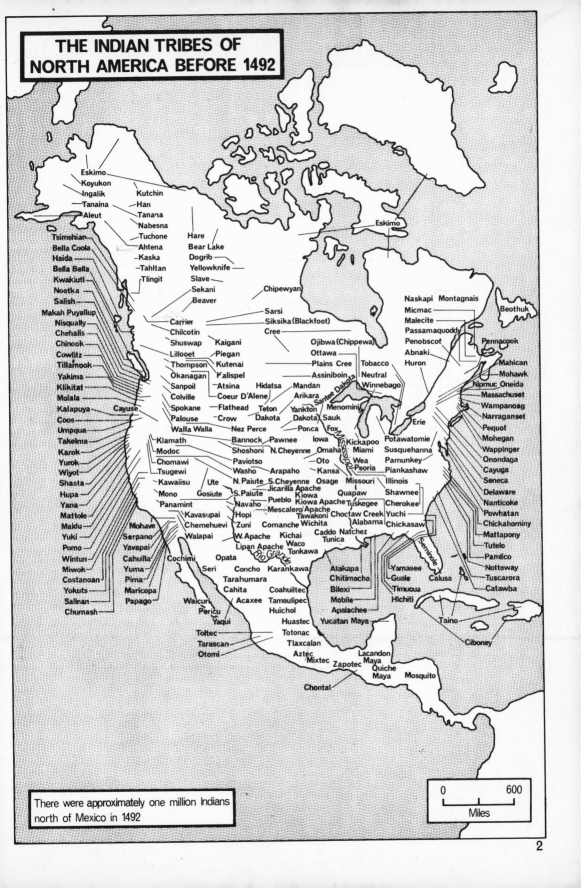

THE INDIAN TRIBES OF NORTH AMERICA BEFORE 1492

Eskimo
Koyukon
Ingalik
Tanaina
Aleut

Kutchin
Han
Tanana
Nabesna
Tuchone
Ahtena
Kaska
Tahltan
Tlingit

Hare
Bear Lake
Dogrib
Yellowknife
Slave
Sekani
Beaver

Eskimo

Chipewyan

Naskapi Montagnais
Micmac
Malecite
Passamaquoddy
Penobscot
Abnaki
Huron

Beothuk

Pennacook

Tsinshian
Bella Coola
Haida
Bella Bella
Kwakiutl
Nootka
Salish
Makah Puyallup
Nisqually
Chehalis
Chinook
Cowlitz
Tillamook
Yakima
Klikitat
Molala
Kalapuya
Coos
Umpqua
Takelma
Karok
Yurok
Wiyot
Shasta
Hupa
Yana
Mattole
Maidu
Yuki
Pomo
Wintun
Miwok
Costanoan
Yokuts
Salinan
Chumash

Carrier
Chilcotin
Shuswap
Lillooet
Thompson
Okanagan
Sanpoil
Colville
Spokane
Palouse
Walla Walla

Cayuse

Klamath
Modoc
Chomawi
Tsugewi
Kawaiisu
Mono
Panamint

Kaigani
Piegan
Kutenai
Kalispel
Atsina
Coeur D'Alene
Flathead
Teton
Dakota
Crow
Nez Perce

Bannock
Shoshoni
Paviotso
Washo

Ute
Gosiute

Sarsi
Siksika (Blackfoot)
Cree

Ojibwa (Chippewa)
Ottawa
Plains Cree
Assiniboin

Hidatsa
Mandan
Arikara
Yankton
Dakota
Ponca

Tobacco
Neutral
Winnebago

Santee Dakota
Menomini
Sauk
Fox

Erie

Pawnee
N.Cheyenne
Arapaho

Iowa
Omaha
Oto
Kansa

Kickapoo
Miami
Wea
Peoria

Potawatomie
Susquehanna
Pamunkey
Piankashaw

Mahican
Mohawk
Nipmuc Oneida
Massachuset
Wampanoag
Narraganset
Pequot
Mohegan
Wappinger
Onondaga
Cayuga
Seneca
Delaware
Nanticoke
Powhatan
Chickahominy
Mattapony
Tutelo
Pamlico
Nottoway
Tuscarora
Catawba

Kavasupai
Chemehuevi
Walapai

Mohave
Serpano
Yavapai
Cahuilla
Yuma
Pima
Maricopa
Papago

Cochimi

Seri

N.Paiute
S.Paiute
Navaho
Hopi
Zuni

Opata
Concho
Tarahumara
Cahita
Acaxee
Huichol

Walcuri
Pericu
Yaqui

Toltec
Tarascan
Otomi

S.Cheyenne
Jicarilla Apache
Kiowa
Pueblo
Mescalero Apache
Comanche
W.Apache
Lipan Apache
Kichai

Osage
Missouri
Kiowa Apache
Tawakoni
Wichita

Quapaw
Choctaw
Caddo Natchez
Tunica

Illinois
Shawnee
Cherokee
Yuchi
Creek
Alabama
Chickasaw

Tuskegee

Waco
Tonkawa

Karankawa
Coahuiltec
Tamaulipec

Atakapa
Chitimacha
Biloxi
Mobile
Apalachee

Yamasee
Guale
Timucua
Hichiti

Seminole

Calusa

Taino

Ciboney

Mosquito

Huastec
Totonac
Tlaxcalan
Aztec
Mixtec
Zapotec

Lacandon
Maya
Quiche
Maya

Chontal

Yucatan Maya

Mississippi

Rio Grande

There were approximately one million Indians
north of Mexico in 1492

0   600
Miles

2

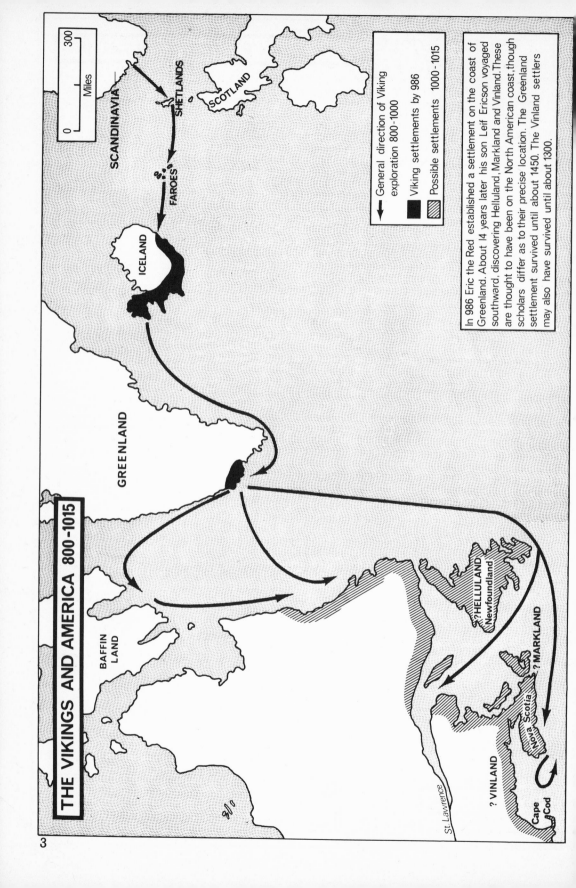

THE VIKINGS AND AMERICA 800-1015

SCANDINAVIA

SHETLANDS

SCOTLAND

FAROES

ICELAND

GREENLAND

BAFFIN LAND

?HELLULAND
Newfoundland

?MARKLAND

Nova Scotia

? VINLAND

St. Lawrence

Cape Cod

0 — 300 Miles

General direction of Viking exploration 800-1000

Viking settlements by 986

Possible settlements 1000-1015

In 986 Eric the Red established a settlement on the coast of Greenland. About 14 years later his son Leif Ericson voyaged southward, discovering Helluland, Markland and Vinland. These are thought to have been on the North American coast, though scholars differ as to their precise location. The Greenland settlement survived until about 1450. The Vinland settlers may also have survived until about 1300.

3

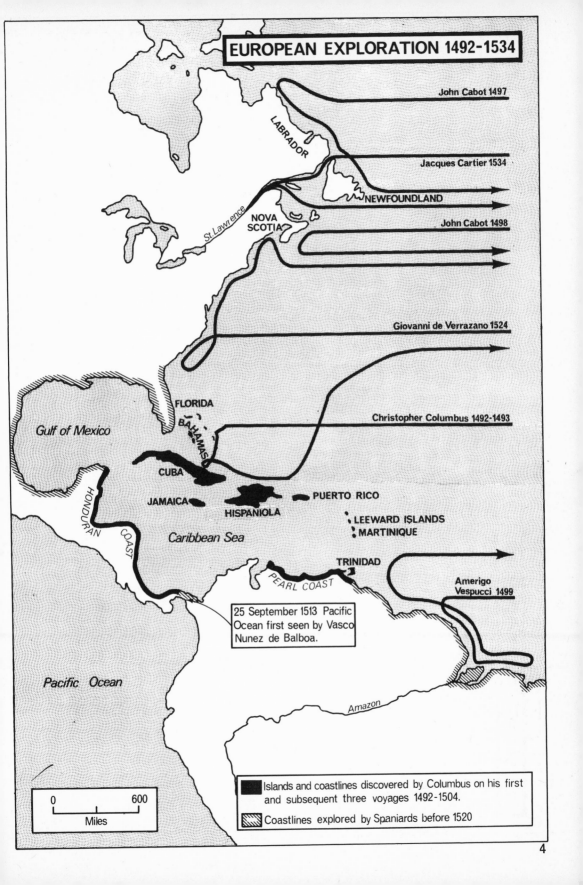

EUROPEAN EXPLORATION 1492-1534

John Cabot 1497

Jacques Cartier 1534

LABRADOR

NEWFOUNDLAND

John Cabot 1498

St. Lawrence

NOVA
SCOTIA

Giovanni de Verrazano 1524

FLORIDA

BAHAMAS

Gulf of Mexico

Christopher Columbus 1492-1493

CUBA

JAMAICA

PUERTO RICO

HISPANIOLA

LEEWARD ISLANDS

MARTINIQUE

HONDURAN COAST

Caribbean Sea

TRINIDAD

PEARL COAST

Amerigo
Vespucci 1499

25 September 1513 Pacific
Ocean first seen by Vasco
Nunez de Balboa.

Pacific Ocean

Amazon

0   600
Miles

Islands and coastlines discovered by Columbus on his first
and subsequent three voyages 1492-1504.

Coastlines explored by Spaniards before 1520

4

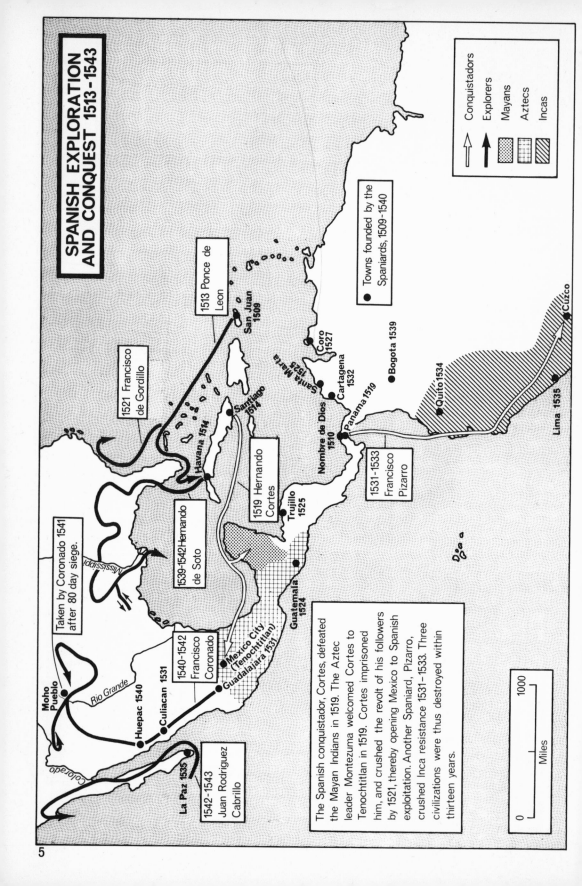

SPANISH EXPLORATION AND CONQUEST 1513–1543

Conquistadors
Explorers
Mayans
Aztecs
Incas

● Towns founded by the Spaniards, 1509–1540

1513 Ponce de Leon

San Juan 1509

1521 Francisco de Gordillo

Coro 1527

Santa Maria 1525

Cartagena 1532

● Bogota 1539

Panama 1519

Nombre de Dios 1510

Quito 1534

Lima 1535

Cuzco

1531–1533 Francisco Pizarro

Havana 1514

Santiago 1514

1519 Hernando Cortes

Trujillo 1525

Guatemala 1524

Mississippi

Taken by Coronado 1541 after 80 day siege.

1539–1542 Hernando de Soto

1540–1542 Francisco Coronado

Culiacan 1531

Mexico City (Tenochtitlan)
Guadalajara 1531

Moho Pueblo

Rio Grande

Huepac 1540

Colorado

La Paz 1535

1542–1543 Juan Rodriguez Cabrillo

The Spanish conquistador, Cortes, defeated the Mayan Indians in 1519. The Aztec leader Montezuma welcomed Cortes to Tenochtitlan in 1519. Cortes imprisoned him, and crushed the revolt of his followers by 1521, thereby opening Mexico to Spanish exploitation. Another Spaniard, Pizarro, crushed Inca resistance 1531–1533. Three civilizations were thus destroyed within thirteen years.

0   Miles   1000

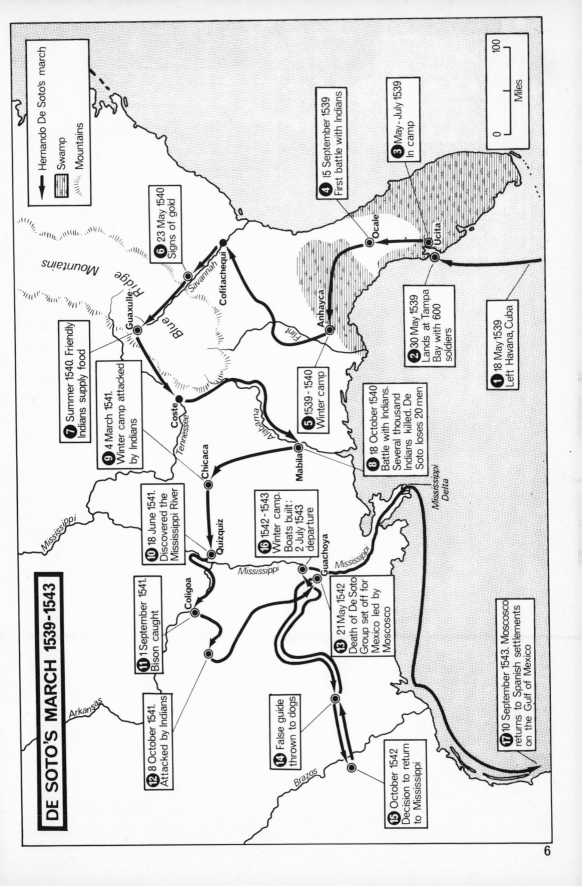

DE SOTO'S MARCH 1539-1543

Key:
- ↓ Hernando De Soto's march
- Swamp
- Mountains

Miles 0 — 100

1 18 May 1539 Left Havana, Cuba

2 30 May 1539 Lands at Tampa Bay with 600 soldiers

3 May–July 1539 In camp

4 15 September 1539 First battle with Indians

5 1539–1540 Winter camp

6 23 May 1540 Signs of gold

7 Summer 1540. Friendly Indians supply food

8 18 October 1540 Battle with Indians. Several thousand Indians killed. De Soto loses 20 men

9 4 March 1541. Winter camp attacked by Indians

10 18 June 1541. Discovered the Mississippi River

11 1 September 1541. Bison caught

12 8 October 1541. Attacked by Indians

13 21 May 1542 Death of De Soto Group set off for Mexico led by Moscosco

14 False guide thrown to dogs

15 October 1542 Decision to return to Mississippi

16 1542–1543 Winter camp. Boats built: 2 July 1543 departure

17 10 September 1543. Moscosco returns to Spanish settlements on the Gulf of Mexico

Place names: Ucita, Ocale, Anhayca, Cofitachequi, Savannah, Guaxulle, Coste, Chicaca, Mabila, Quizquiz, Coligoa, Guachoya

Rivers/features: Mississippi, Arkansas, Brazos, Flint, Alatama, Tennessee, Mississippi Delta, Blue Ridge Mountains, Mountains

6

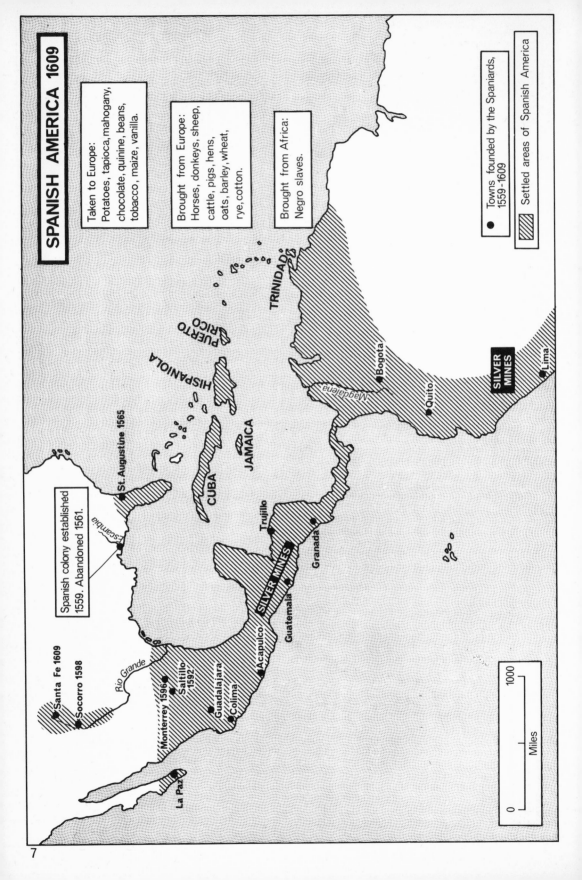

SPANISH AMERICA 1609

Taken to Europe:
Potatoes, tapioca, mahogany, chocolate, quinine, beans, tobacco, maize, vanilla.

Brought from Europe:
Horses, donkeys, sheep, cattle, pigs, hens, oats, barley, wheat, rye, cotton.

Brought from Africa:
Negro slaves.

● Towns founded by the Spaniards, 1559-1609

Settled areas of Spanish America

TRINIDAD

PUERTO RICO

HISPANIOLA

SILVER MINES

●Bogota

●Quito

●Lima

Magdalena

St. Augustine 1565

Spanish colony established 1559. Abandoned 1561.

Escambia

JAMAICA

CUBA

Truillo

Granada●

SILVER MINES

Guatemala●

Acapulco●

Santa Fe 1609

Socorro 1598

Rio Grande

Monterrey 1596

Saltillo 1592

Guadalajara●

Colima●

La Paz

0   1000

Miles

7

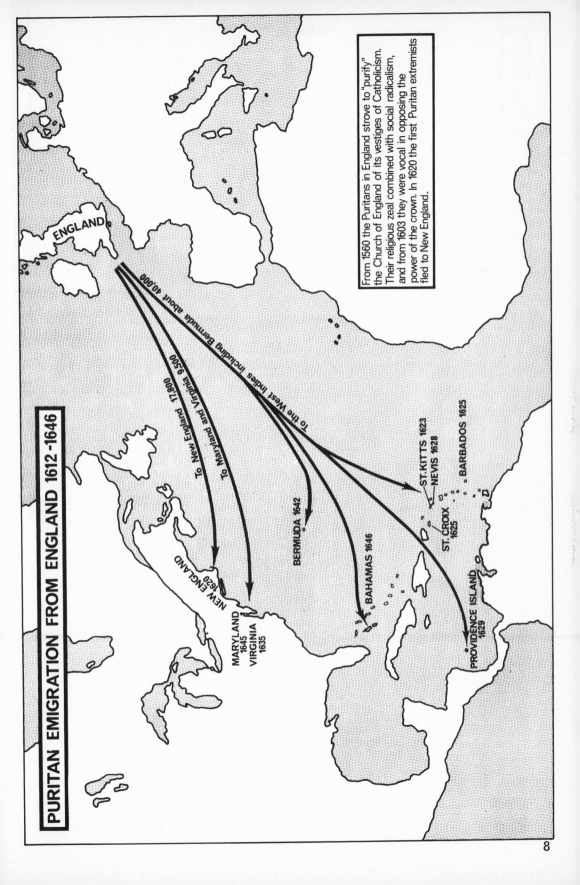

PURITAN EMIGRATION FROM ENGLAND 1612-1646

ENGLAND

From 1560 the Puritans in England strove to "purify" the Church of England of its vestiges of Catholicism. Their religious zeal combined with social radicalism, and from 1603 they were vocal in opposing the power of the crown. In 1620 the first Puritan extremists fled to New England.

To the West Indies including Bermuda about 40,000

To New England 17,800

To Maryland and Virginia 9,500

NEW ENGLAND

MARYLAND 1645
VIRGINIA 1635

BERMUDA 1642

BAHAMAS 1646

ST. KITTS 1623
NEVIS 1628

BARBADOS 1625

ST. CROIX 1625

PROVIDENCE ISLAND 1629

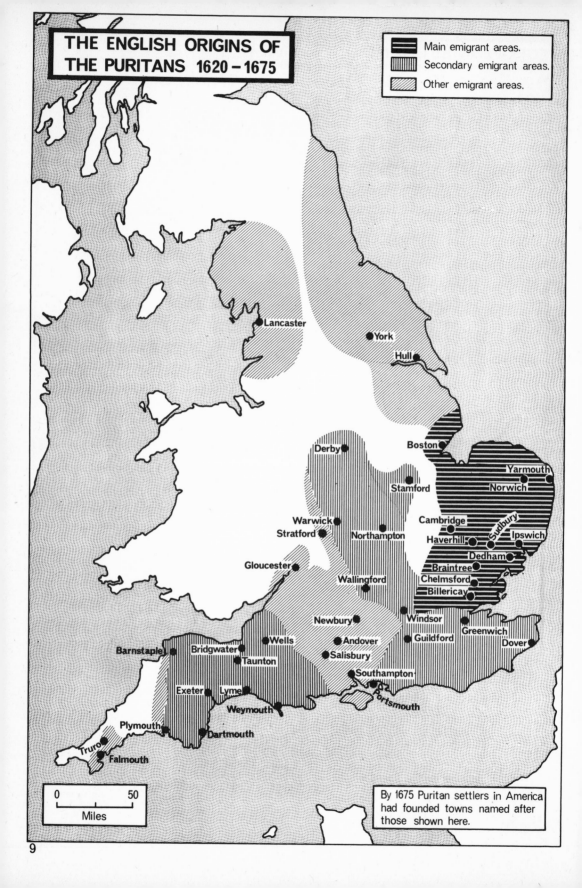

THE ENGLISH ORIGINS OF THE PURITANS 1620 – 1675

Legend:
- Main emigrant areas.
- Secondary emigrant areas.
- Other emigrant areas.

Lancaster

York

Hull

Derby

Boston

Yarmouth

Stamford

Norwich

Warwick

Cambridge

Stratford

Northampton

Haverhill

Sudbury

Ipswich

Dedham

Gloucester

Braintree

Wallingford

Chelmsford

Billericay

Newbury

Windsor

Greenwich

Wells

Andover

Guildford

Dover

Barnstaple

Bridgwater

Salisbury

Taunton

Southampton

Exeter

Lyme

Portsmouth

Weymouth

Plymouth

Dartmouth

Truro

Falmouth

0   50

Miles

By 1675 Puritan settlers in America had founded towns named after those shown here.

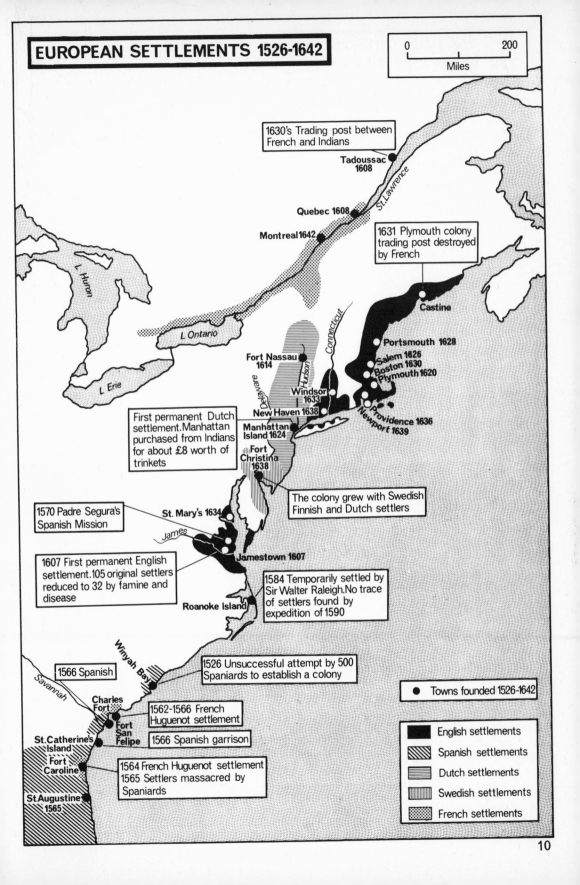

EUROPEAN SETTLEMENTS 1526-1642

0   200

Miles

1630's Trading post between French and Indians

Tadoussac 1608

St.Lawrence

Quebec 1608

Montreal 1642

1631 Plymouth colony trading post destroyed by French

L. Huron

L. Ontario

L. Erie

Castine

Fort Nassau 1614

Hudson

Connecticut

Portsmouth 1628

Salem 1626
Boston 1630
Plymouth 1620

Windsor 1633

Delaware

New Haven 1638

Providence 1636

Newport 1639

First permanent Dutch settlement. Manhattan purchased from Indians for about £8 worth of trinkets

Manhattan Island 1624

Fort Christina 1638

The colony grew with Swedish Finnish and Dutch settlers

1570 Padre Segura's Spanish Mission

St. Mary's 1634

James

1607 First permanent English settlement.105 original settlers reduced to 32 by famine and disease

Jamestown 1607

1584 Temporarily settled by Sir Walter Raleigh. No trace of settlers found by expedition of 1590

Roanoke Island

Winyah Bay

1526 Unsuccessful attempt by 500 Spaniards to establish a colony

Savannah

1566 Spanish

Charles Fort

1562-1566 French Huguenot settlement

Fort San Felipe

St.Catherine's Island

1566 Spanish garrison

Fort Caroline

1564 French Huguenot settlement 1565 Settlers massacred by Spaniards

St.Augustine 1565

● Towns founded 1526-1642

●	Towns founded 1526-1642
■	English settlements
▨	Spanish settlements
▤	Dutch settlements
▥	Swedish settlements
▦	French settlements

10

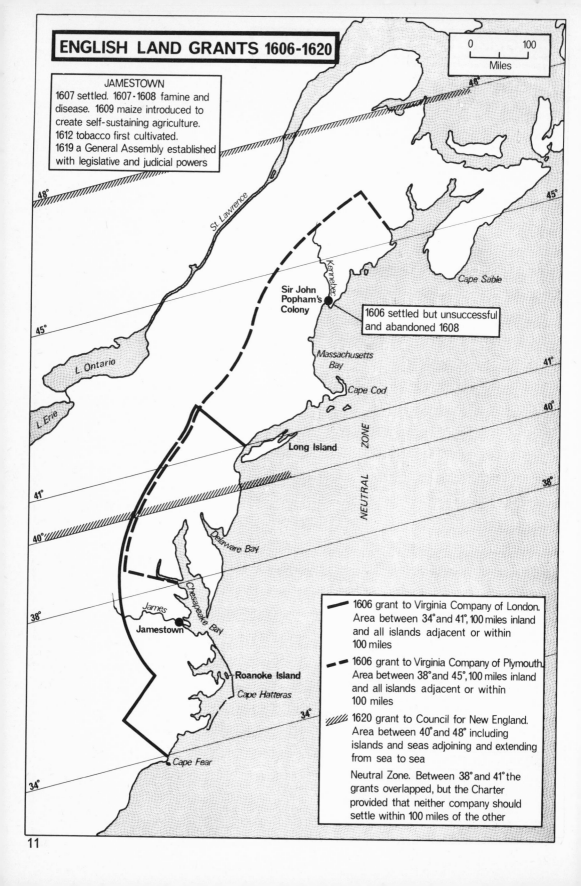

ENGLISH LAND GRANTS 1606-1620

0   100
Miles

JAMESTOWN
1607 settled. 1607-1608 famine and disease. 1609 maize introduced to create self-sustaining agriculture. 1612 tobacco first cultivated. 1619 a General Assembly established with legislative and judicial powers

48°
45°

St. Lawrence

Sir John Popham's Colony

1606 settled but unsuccessful and abandoned 1608

Cape Sable

45°

L Ontario

Massachusetts Bay

41°

L Erie

Cape Cod

40°

Long Island

NEUTRAL ZONE

38°

41°

Delaware Bay

40°

38°

James
Jamestown

Chesapeake Bay

—— 1606 grant to Virginia Company of London. Area between 34° and 41°, 100 miles inland and all islands adjacent or within 100 miles

– – 1606 grant to Virginia Company of Plymouth. Area between 38° and 45°, 100 miles inland and all islands adjacent or within 100 miles

Roanoke Island

Cape Hatteras

34°

/////// 1620 grant to Council for New England. Area between 40° and 48° including islands and seas adjoining and extending from sea to sea

Cape Fear

34°

Neutral Zone. Between 38° and 41° the grants overlapped, but the Charter provided that neither company should settle within 100 miles of the other

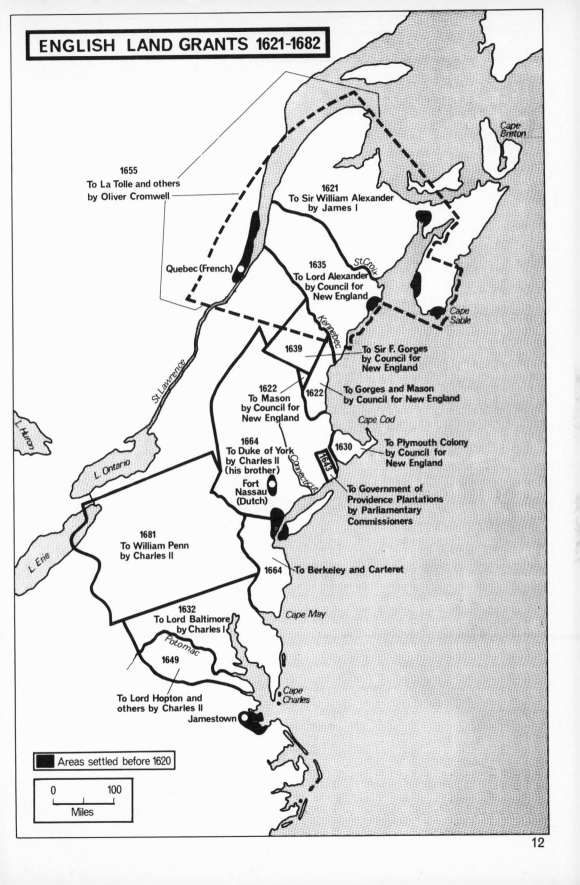

ENGLISH LAND GRANTS 1621-1682

1655
To La Tolle and others by Oliver Cromwell

1621
To Sir William Alexander by James I

Cape Breton

1635
To Lord Alexander by Council for New England

St Croix

Quebec (French)

Kennebec

Cape Sable

1639

1622
To Mason by Council for New England

1622

To Sir F. Gorges by Council for New England

To Gorges and Mason by Council for New England

Cape Cod

L. Huron

1664
To Duke of York by Charles II (his brother)

1630

To Plymouth Colony by Council for New England

L. Ontario

Fort Nassau (Dutch)

Connecticut

1643

To Government of Providence Plantations by Parliamentary Commissioners

1681
To William Penn by Charles II

L. Erie

1664 **To Berkeley and Carteret**

Cape May

1632
To Lord Baltimore by Charles I

Potomac

1649

To Lord Hopton and others by Charles II

Jamestown

Cape Charles

St. Lawrence

■ Areas settled before 1620

0   100
Miles

12

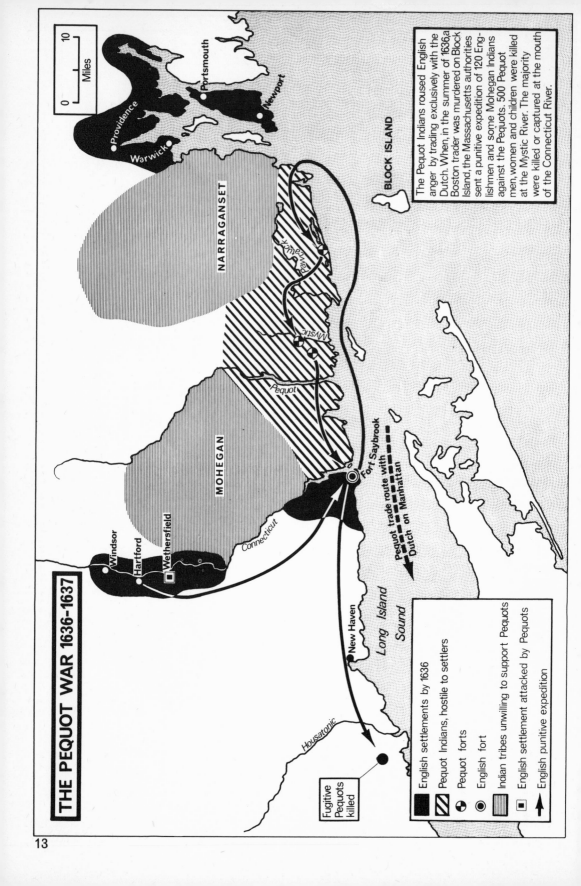

THE PEQUOT WAR 1636-1637

The Pequot Indians roused English anger by trading exclusively with the Dutch. When, in the summer of 1636, a Boston trader was murdered on Block Island, the Massachusetts authorities sent a punitive expedition of 120 Englishmen and some Mohegan Indians against the Pequots. 500 Pequot men, women and children were killed at the Mystic River. The majority were killed or captured at the mouth of the Connecticut River.

0 10
Miles

Providence
Warwick
Portsmouth
Newport

BLOCK ISLAND

NARRAGANSET

Pawcatuck

MYSTIC

Pequot

MOHEGAN

Windsor
Hartford
Wethersfield

Connecticut

Fort Saybrook

Pequot trade route with
Dutch on Manhattan

New Haven

Long Island Sound

Housatonic

Fugitive
Pequots
killed

■ English settlements by 1636
▨ Pequot Indians, hostile to settlers
⊕ Pequot forts
◉ English fort
▥ Indian tribes unwilling to support Pequots
▣ English settlement attacked by Pequots
➤ English punitive expedition

13

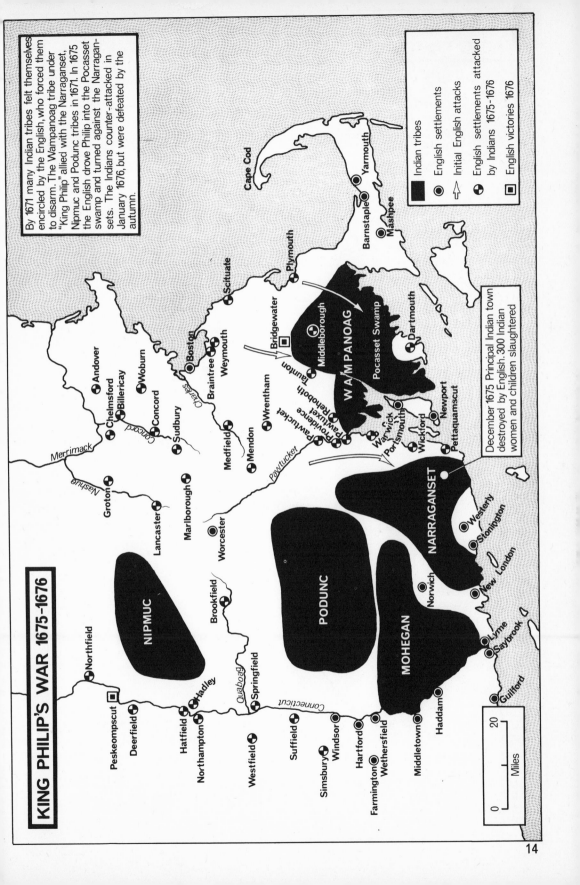

KING PHILIP'S WAR 1675-1676

By 1671 many Indian tribes felt themselves encircled by the English, who forced them to disarm. The Wampanoag tribe under "King Philip" allied with the Narraganset, Nipmuc and Podunc tribes in 1671. In 1675 the English drove Philip into the Pocasset swamp and turned against the Narragansets. The Indians counter-attacked in January 1676, but were defeated by the autumn.

Legend:
- ■ Indian tribes
- ◉ English settlements
- ⇧ Initial English attacks
- ◕ English settlements attacked by Indians 1675-1676
- ▣ English victories 1676

December 1675 Principal Indian town destroyed by English. 300 Indian women and children slaughtered

Tribes: NIPMUC, PODUNC, WAMPANOAG, NARRAGANSET, MOHEGAN

Place names:
Northfield, Peskeompscut, Deerfield, Hadley, Hatfield, Northampton, Westfield, Suffield, Springfield, Brookfield, Worcester, Marlborough, Lancaster, Groton, Nashua, Merrimack, Andover, Chelmsford, Billericay, Woburn, Concord, Sudbury, Boston, Braintree, Weymouth, Scituate, Plymouth, Barnstaple, Mashpee, Yarmouth, Cape Cod, Dartmouth, Pocasset Swamp, Middleborough, Bridgewater, Taunton, Rehoboth, Wrentham, Mendon, Medfield, Pawtuxet, Providence, Pawtucket, Warwick, Portsmouth, Newport, Pettaquamscut, Wickford, Westerly, Stonington, New London, Norwich, Lyme, Saybrook, Guilford, Haddam, Middletown, Wethersfield, Hartford, Windsor, Simsbury, Farmington

Rivers: Merrimack, Nashua, Concord, Charles, Pawtucket, Quaboag, Connecticut

Scale: 0 — 20 Miles

14

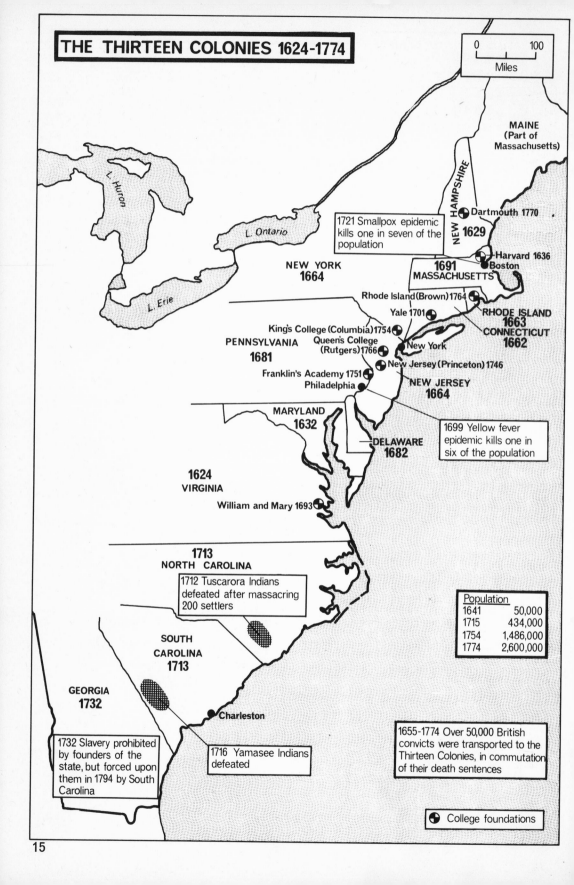

THE THIRTEEN COLONIES 1624-1774

0   100
Miles

MAINE
(Part of
Massachusetts)

NEW HAMPSHIRE
1629

● Dartmouth 1770

1721 Smallpox epidemic kills one in seven of the population

1691
MASSACHUSETTS

● Harvard 1636
● Boston

NEW YORK
1664

Rhode Island(Brown) 1764 ●

Yale 1701 ●

RHODE ISLAND
1663
CONNECTICUT
1662

King's College (Columbia) 1754 ●
PENNSYLVANIA   Queen's College
1681   (Rutgers) 1766 ●

● New York

● New Jersey (Princeton) 1746

Franklin's Academy 1751 ●
● Philadelphia

NEW JERSEY
1664

MARYLAND
1632

● DELAWARE
1682

1699 Yellow fever epidemic kills one in six of the population

1624
VIRGINIA

William and Mary 1693 ●

1713
NORTH CAROLINA

1712 Tuscarora Indians defeated after massacring 200 settlers

Population	
1641	50,000
1715	434,000
1754	1,486,000
1774	2,600,000

SOUTH
CAROLINA
1713

GEORGIA
1732

● Charleston

1732 Slavery prohibited by founders of the state, but forced upon them in 1794 by South Carolina

1716 Yamasee Indians defeated

1655-1774 Over 50,000 British convicts were transported to the Thirteen Colonies, in commutation of their death sentences

L. Huron

L. Ontario

L. Erie

● College foundations

15

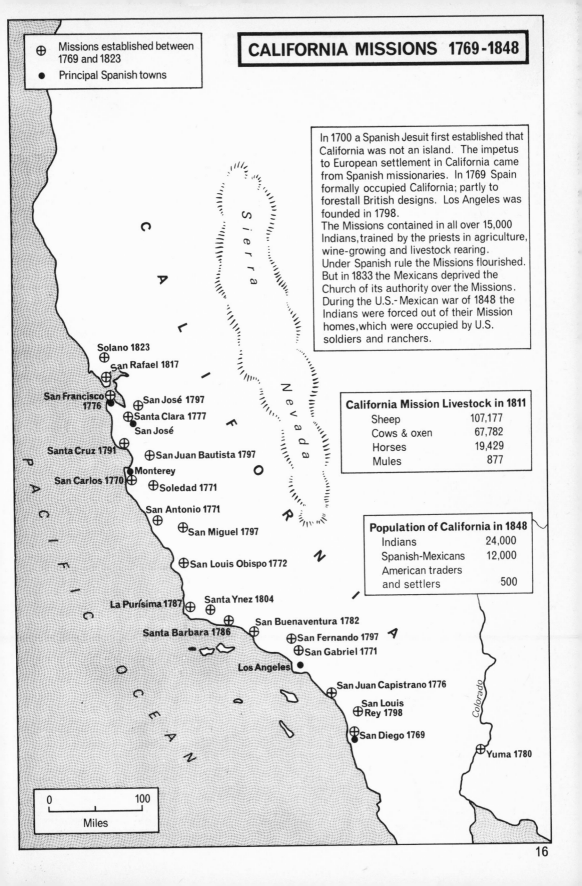

CALIFORNIA MISSIONS 1769-1848

⊕ Missions established between 1769 and 1823

● Principal Spanish towns

In 1700 a Spanish Jesuit first established that California was not an island. The impetus to European settlement in California came from Spanish missionaries. In 1769 Spain formally occupied California; partly to forestall British designs. Los Angeles was founded in 1798.

The Missions contained in all over 15,000 Indians, trained by the priests in agriculture, wine-growing and livestock rearing.

Under Spanish rule the Missions flourished. But in 1833 the Mexicans deprived the Church of its authority over the Missions. During the U.S.-Mexican war of 1848 the Indians were forced out of their Mission homes, which were occupied by U.S. soldiers and ranchers.

California Mission Livestock in 1811

Sheep	107,177
Cows & oxen	67,782
Horses	19,429
Mules	877

Population of California in 1848

Indians	24,000
Spanish-Mexicans	12,000
American traders and settlers	500

Sierra

Nevada

C A L I F O R N I A

PACIFIC OCEAN

Solano 1823
San Rafael 1817
San Francisco 1776
San José 1797
Santa Clara 1777
San José
Santa Cruz 1791
San Juan Bautista 1797
Monterey
San Carlos 1770
Soledad 1771
San Antonio 1771
San Miguel 1797
San Louis Obispo 1772
La Purísima 1787
Santa Ynez 1804
Santa Barbara 1786
San Buenaventura 1782
San Fernando 1797
San Gabriel 1771
Los Angeles
San Juan Capistrano 1776
San Louis Rey 1798
San Diego 1769
Yuma 1780

Colorado

0   100
Miles

16

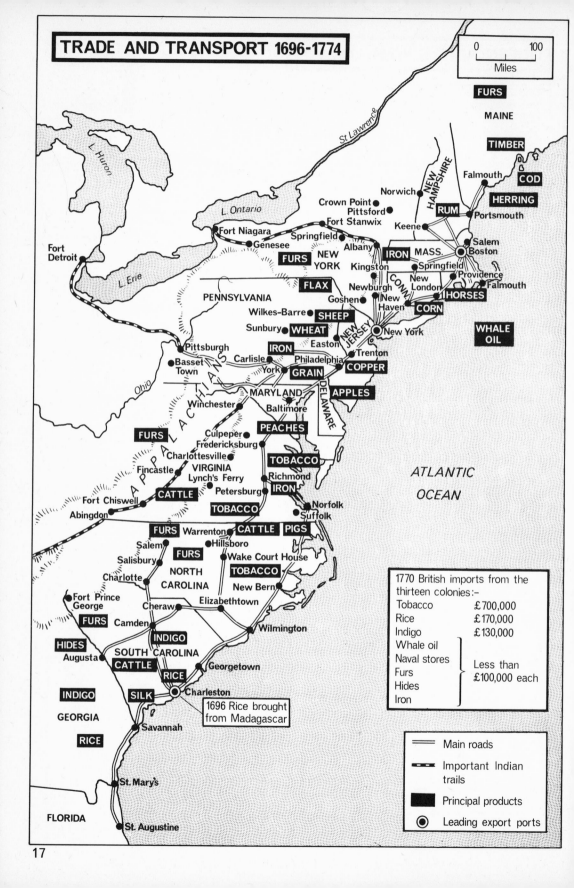

TRADE AND TRANSPORT 1696-1774

0 ___ 100
Miles

FURS
MAINE

TIMBER

COD

L. Huron

St Lawrence

Norwich
Crown Point
Pittsford
Fort Stanwix
L. Ontario
Fort Niagara
Genesee
Springfield
Albany
Keene
Kingston
NEW HAMPSHIRE
RUM
Falmouth
Portsmouth
HERRING
Salem
Boston
MASS.
IRON
Springfield
New London
New Haven
Newburgh
Goshen
FURS NEW YORK
CORN
HORSES
Providence
Falmouth
WHALE OIL

Fort Detroit
L. Erie

PENNSYLVANIA
FLAX
Wilkes-Barre
Sunbury
SHEEP
WHEAT
Easton
NEW JERSEY
New York

Pittsburgh
Basset Town
Carlisle
York
IRON
Philadelphia
GRAIN
Trenton
COPPER

Ohio

MARYLAND
Baltimore
DELAWARE
APPLES

Winchester
Culpeper
Fredericksburg
Charlottesville
FURS
PEACHES

Fincastle
VIRGINIA
Lynch's Ferry
Richmond
Petersburg
TOBACCO
IRON

Fort Chiswell
CATTLE
TOBACCO
Norfolk
Suffolk

Abingdon
Warrenton
FURS
CATTLE
PIGS

ATLANTIC OCEAN

APPALACHIANS

Salem
Hillsboro
Salisbury
FURS
Wake Court House
Charlotte
NORTH CAROLINA
TOBACCO
New Bern

Fort Prince George
Cheraw
Elizabethtown
Wilmington

FURS
Camden
HIDES
Augusta
INDIGO
SOUTH CAROLINA
CATTLE
RICE
Georgetown

INDIGO
SILK
Charleston
Savannah
GEORGIA
RICE

1696 Rice brought from Madagascar

1770 British imports from the thirteen colonies:-	
Tobacco	£700,000
Rice	£170,000
Indigo	£130,000
Whale oil	
Naval stores	
Furs	Less than £100,000 each
Hides	
Iron	

St. Mary's

FLORIDA
St. Augustine

═══	Main roads
▬▬▬	Important Indian trails
■	Principal products
◉	Leading export ports

17

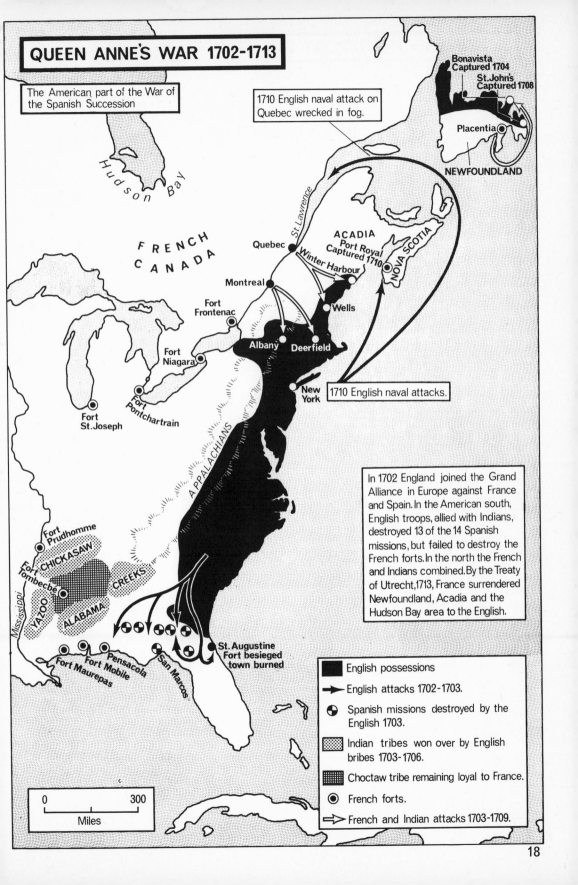

QUEEN ANNE'S WAR 1702-1713

The American part of the War of the Spanish Succession

1710 English naval attack on Quebec wrecked in fog.

Bonavista Captured 1704
St. John's Captured 1708
Placentia
NEWFOUNDLAND

Hudson Bay

F R E N C H
C A N A D A

St. Lawrence

ACADIA
Port Royal Captured 1710

Quebec
Winter Harbour
NOVA SCOTIA

Montreal
Wells

Fort Frontenac

Albany   Deerfield

Fort Niagara

Fort Pontchartrain

New York

1710 English naval attacks.

Fort St. Joseph

APPALACHIANS

In 1702 England joined the Grand Alliance in Europe against France and Spain. In the American south, English troops, allied with Indians, destroyed 13 of the 14 Spanish missions, but failed to destroy the French forts. In the north the French and Indians combined. By the Treaty of Utrecht, 1713, France surrendered Newfoundland, Acadia and the Hudson Bay area to the English.

Fort Prudhomme
CHICKASAW
Fort Tombecbe
CREEKS
Mississippi
YAZOO
ALABAMA

Pensacola
Fort Mobile
Fort Maurepas
San Marcos

St. Augustine Fort besieged town burned

	English possessions
→	English attacks 1702-1703.
✪	Spanish missions destroyed by the English 1703.
▦	Indian tribes won over by English bribes 1703-1706.
▩	Choctaw tribe remaining loyal to France.
⊙	French forts.
⇨	French and Indian attacks 1703-1709.

0   300
Miles

18

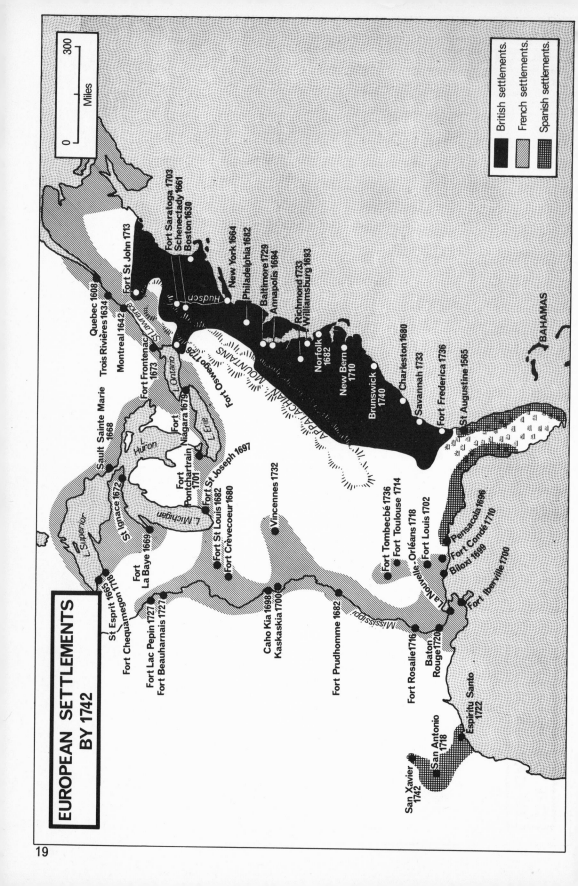

EUROPEAN SETTLEMENTS BY 1742

300
Miles
0

British settlements.
French settlements.
Spanish settlements.

BAHAMAS

Fort Saratoga 1703
Schenectady 1661
Boston 1630
New York 1664
Philadelphia 1682
Baltimore 1729
Annapolis 1694
Richmond 1733
Williamsburg 1693
Norfolk 1682
Charleston 1680
New Bern 1710
Savannah 1733
Brunswick 1740
Fort Frederica 1736
St Augustine 1565

Quebec 1608
Montreal 1642
Trois Rivières 1634
Fort St John 1713
Fort Frontenac 1673
Fort Oswego 1726
Hudson
St Lawrence
L. Ontario
L. Erie
APPALACHIAN MOUNTAINS

Sault Sainte Marie 1668
St Ignace 1672
Fort Pontchartrain 1701
Fort Niagara 1679
Fort St Joseph 1697
L. Huron
L. Michigan
Fort
St Esprit 1665
Fort Chequamegon 1718
Fort La Baye 1669
Fort Lac Pepin 1727
Fort Beauharnais 1727
Fort St Louis 1682
Fort Crèvecoeur 1680
Vincennes 1732
Caho Kia 1698
Kaskaskia 1700
Fort Prudhomme 1682
L. Superior

Fort Tombecbé 1736
Fort Toulouse 1714
La Nouvelle- Orléans 1718
Fort Louis 1702
Pensacola 1696
Fort Condé 1710
Biloxi 1699
Fort Iberville 1700
La Mobile
Mississippi

Fort Rosalie 1716
Baton Rouge 1720

Espiritu Santo 1722

San Antonio 1718
San Xavier 1742

19

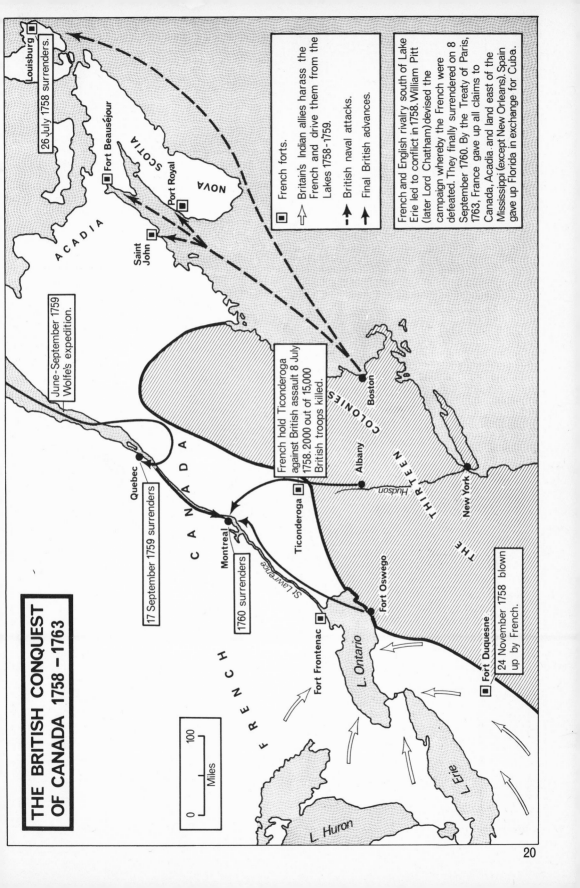

THE BRITISH CONQUEST OF CANADA 1758 – 1763

French and English rivalry south of Lake Erie led to conflict in 1758. William Pitt (later Lord Chatham) devised the campaign whereby the French were defeated. They finally surrendered on 8 September 1760. By the Treaty of Paris, 1763, France gave up all claims to Canada, Acadia and land east of the Mississippi (except New Orleans). Spain gave up Florida in exchange for Cuba.

■ French forts.

⇨ Britain's Indian allies harass the French and drive them from the Lakes 1758-1759.

◀‑ ‑ British naval attacks.

◀— Final British advances.

Louisburg surrenders.
26 July 1758 surrenders.

June-September 1759 Wolfe's expedition.

17 September 1759 surrenders.

1760 surrenders.

French hold Ticonderoga against British assault 8 July 1758. 2000 out of 15,000 British troops killed.

24 November 1758 blown up by French.

Fort Beauséjour

Port Royal

Saint John

NOVA SCOTIA

ACADIA

CANADA

FRENCH

Quebec

Montreal

Ticonderoga

Albany

Boston

New York

Hudson

THE THIRTEEN COLONIES

St. Lawrence

Fort Frontenac

Fort Oswego

Fort Duquesne

L. Ontario

L. Erie

L. Huron

0   100
Miles

20

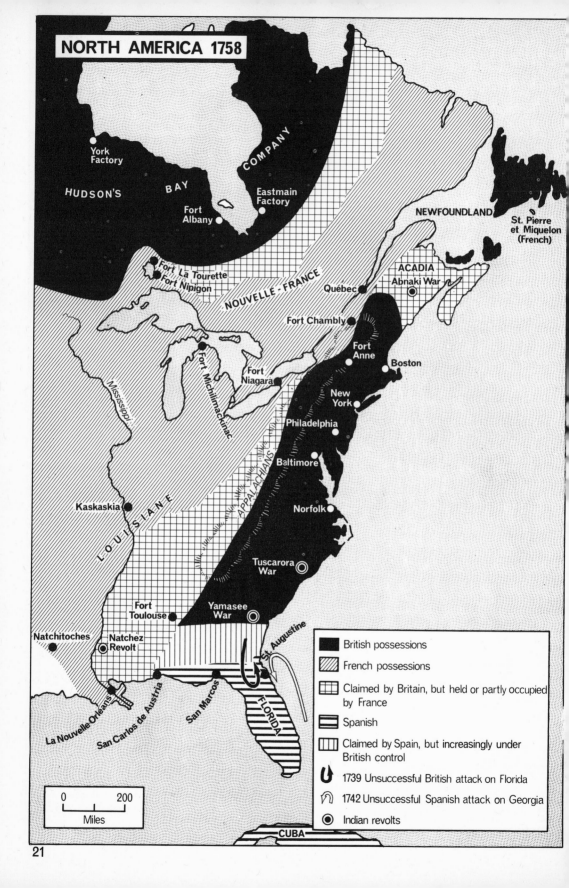

NORTH AMERICA 1758

HUDSON'S BAY COMPANY

York Factory

Fort Albany

Eastmain Factory

NEWFOUNDLAND

St. Pierre et Miquelon (French)

Fort La Tourette
Fort Nipigon

NOUVELLE - FRANCE

Québec

ACADIA
Abnaki War

Fort Chambly

Fort Michilimackinac

Fort Anne

Boston

Fort Niagara

New York

Philadelphia

Baltimore

MISSISSIPPI

APPALACHIANS

LOUISIANE

Kaskaskia

Norfolk

Tuscarora War

Fort Toulouse

Yamasee War

Natchitoches

Natchez Revolt

La Nouvelle-Orléans

San Carlos de Austria

San Marcos

St. Augustine

FLORIDA

■ British possessions

▨ French possessions

▦ Claimed by Britain, but held or partly occupied by France

▤ Spanish

▥ Claimed by Spain, but increasingly under British control

⨃ 1739 Unsuccessful British attack on Florida

⋔ 1742 Unsuccessful Spanish attack on Georgia

◉ Indian revolts

CUBA

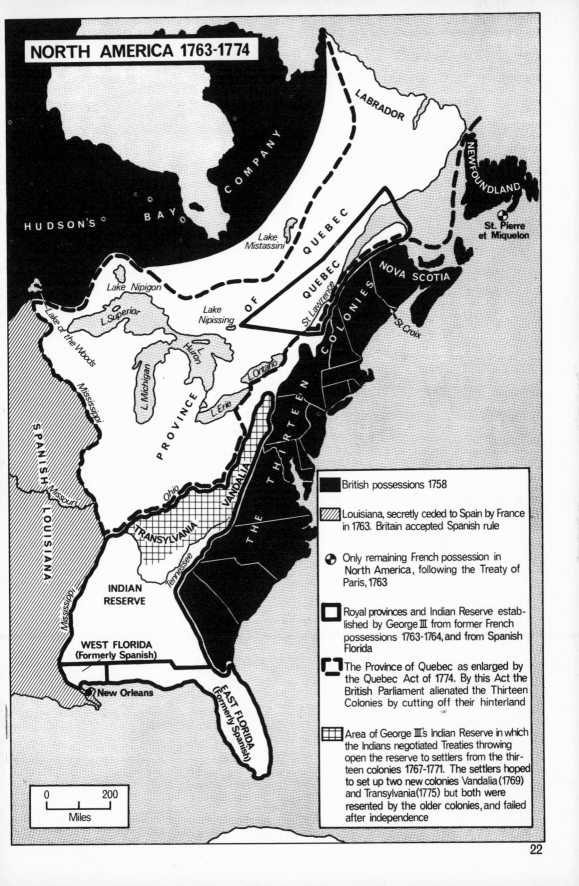

NORTH AMERICA 1763-1774

LABRADOR

NEWFOUNDLAND

HUDSON'S BAY COMPANY

St. Pierre et Miquelon

Lake Mistassini

QUEBEC

PROVINCE OF QUEBEC

NOVA SCOTIA

Lake Nipigon

Lake Nipissing

St.Lawrence

St.Croix

Lake of the Woods

L.Superior

Huron

L.Michigan

Ontario

L.Erie

THE THIRTEEN COLONIES

SPANISH LOUISIANA

Missouri

Mississippi

PROVINCE

Ohio

VANDALIA

TRANSYLVANIA

Tennessee

INDIAN RESERVE

Mississippi

WEST FLORIDA (Formerly Spanish)

New Orleans

EAST FLORIDA (Formerly Spanish)

British possessions 1758

Louisiana, secretly ceded to Spain by France in 1763. Britain accepted Spanish rule

Only remaining French possession in North America, following the Treaty of Paris, 1763

Royal provinces and Indian Reserve established by George III from former French possessions 1763-1764, and from Spanish Florida

The Province of Quebec as enlarged by the Quebec Act of 1774. By this Act the British Parliament alienated the Thirteen Colonies by cutting off their hinterland

Area of George III's Indian Reserve in which the Indians negotiated Treaties throwing open the reserve to settlers from the thirteen colonies 1767-1771. The settlers hoped to set up two new colonies Vandalia (1769) and Transylvania (1775) but both were resented by the older colonies, and failed after independence

0   200
Miles

22

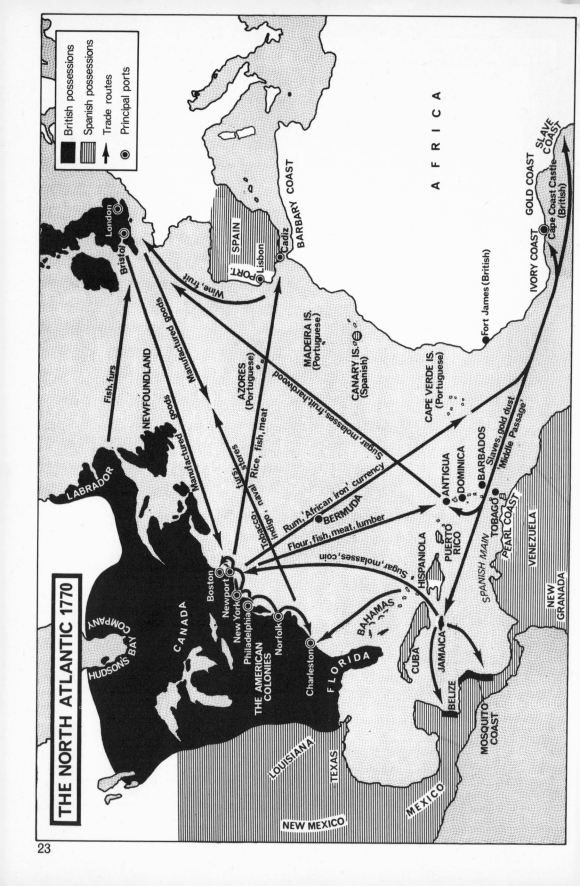

THE NORTH ATLANTIC 1770

Legend:
- British possessions
- Spanish possessions
- Trade routes
- Principal ports

AFRICA

SPAIN

PORT. Lisbon
Cadiz
BARBARY COAST

London
Bristol

GOLD COAST
SLAVE COAST
IVORY COAST

Cape Coast Castle (British)

Fort James (British)

NEWFOUNDLAND

Fish, furs

Manufactured goods

Manufactured goods

Wine, fruit

AZORES (Portuguese)

MADEIRA IS. (Portuguese)

CANARY IS. (Spanish)

CAPE VERDE IS. (Portuguese)

Sugar, molasses, fruit, hardwood

furs, stores

Tobacco, naval, Rice, fish, meat
indigo stores

LABRADOR

Rum, 'African iron', currency

BERMUDA

Flour, fish, meat, lumber

Sugar, molasses, coin

Slaves, gold dust

'Middle Passage'

ANTIGUA
DOMINICA
BARBADOS
TOBAGO
PEARL COAST

PUERTO RICO

HISPANIOLA

SPANISH MAIN

VENEZUELA

NEW GRANADA

HUDSON'S BAY COMPANY

CANADA

Boston
Newport
New York
Philadelphia
Norfolk
Charleston

THE AMERICAN COLONIES

BAHAMAS

CUBA

JAMAICA

FLORIDA

BELIZE

MOSQUITO COAST

LOUISIANA

TEXAS

MEXICO

NEW MEXICO

23

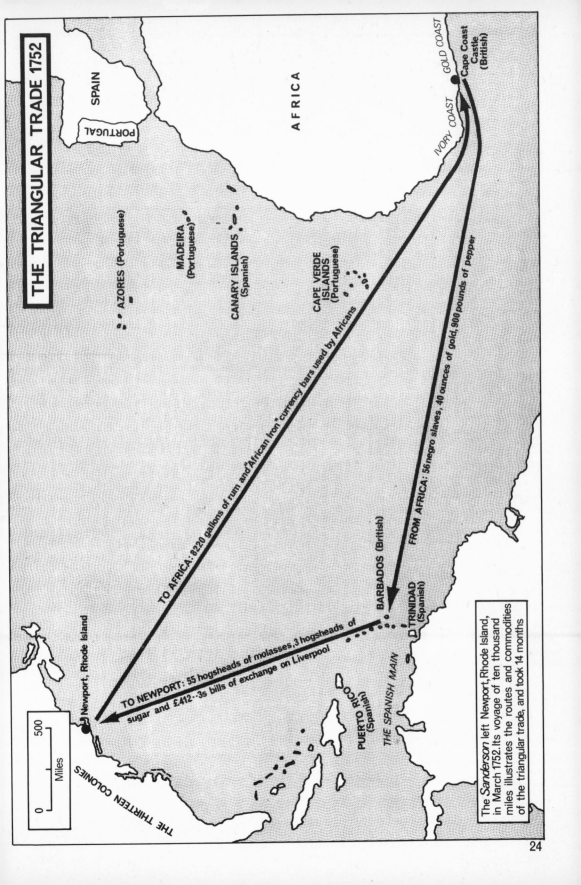

THE TRIANGULAR TRADE 1752

SPAIN

PORTUGAL

AFRICA

GOLD COAST

Cape Coast
Castle
(British)

IVORY COAST

AZORES (Portuguese)

MADEIRA
(Portuguese)

CANARY ISLANDS
(Spanish)

CAPE VERDE
ISLANDS
(Portuguese)

TO AFRICA: 8220 gallons of rum and African iron "currency bars used by Africans

FROM AFRICA: 56 negro slaves, 40 ounces of gold, 900 pounds of pepper

BARBADOS (British)

TRINIDAD (Spanish)

Newport, Rhode Island

TO NEWPORT: 55 hogsheads of molasses, 3 hogsheads of sugar and £412..3s bills of exchange on Liverpool

PUERTO RICO
(Spanish)

THE SPANISH MAIN

THE THIRTEEN COLONIES

500

Miles

0

The *Sanderson* left Newport, Rhode Island, in March 1752. Its voyage of ten thousand miles illustrates the routes and commodities of the triangular trade, and took 14 months

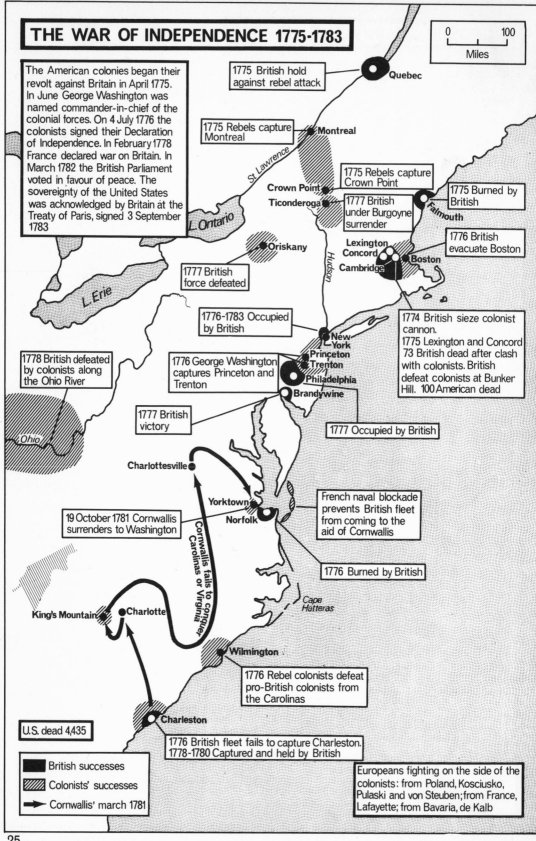

THE WAR OF INDEPENDENCE 1775-1783

0   100
Miles

1775 British hold against rebel attack — Quebec

The American colonies began their revolt against Britain in April 1775. In June George Washington was named commander-in-chief of the colonial forces. On 4 July 1776 the colonists signed their Declaration of Independence. In February 1778 France declared war on Britain. In March 1782 the British Parliament voted in favour of peace. The sovereignty of the United States was acknowledged by Britain at the Treaty of Paris, signed 3 September 1783

1775 Rebels capture Montreal — Montreal

St. Lawrence

1775 Rebels capture Crown Point

Crown Point

Ticonderoga

1777 British under Burgoyne surrender

Falmouth

1775 Burned by British

L. Ontario

L. Erie

Oriskany

1777 British force defeated

Hudson

Lexington
Concord
Cambridge

Boston

1776 British evacuate Boston

1776-1783 Occupied by British

New York
Princeton
Trenton
Philadelphia

**1774 British sieze colonist cannon.
1775 Lexington and Concord 73 British dead after clash with colonists. British defeat colonists at Bunker Hill. 100 American dead**

1776 George Washington captures Princeton and Trenton

Brandywine

1778 British defeated by colonists along the Ohio River

1777 British victory

1777 Occupied by British

Ohio

Charlottesville

Yorktown
Norfolk

French naval blockade prevents British fleet from coming to the aid of Cornwallis

19 October 1781 Cornwallis surrenders to Washington

Cornwallis fails to conquer Carolinas or Virginia

1776 Burned by British

Cape Hatteras

King's Mountain — Charlotte

Wilmington

1776 Rebel colonists defeat pro-British colonists from the Carolinas

U.S. dead 4,435

Charleston

1776 British fleet fails to capture Charleston. 1778-1780 Captured and held by British

- ■ British successes
- ▨ Colonists' successes
- → Cornwallis' march 1781

Europeans fighting on the side of the colonists: from Poland, Kosciusko, Pulaski and von Steuben; from France, Lafayette; from Bavaria, de Kalb

PROPOSED BOUNDARIES 1779-1782

Lake of
the Woods

L.Nipigon

1782 Cession of Canada to
U.S. proposed by Franklin

BRITISH CANADA

Ottawa

St.Lawrence

St Croix

L. Superior

L.Huron

L.
Ontario

NH

L.Michigan

NEW YORK

MASS

RI

Erie

CONN

SPANISH

Country north of
the Ohio River at
the disposal of
England (French
proposal)

PENNSYLVANIA

NJ

DEL

LOUISIANA

Wabash

Ohio

MD

VIRGINIA

ATLANTIC

OCEAN

Mississippi

Tennessee

NORTH
CAROLINA

Indian country under
protection of Spain
(French proposal)

SOUTH
CAROLINA

GEORGIA

Ruled by Britain 1763-1783
Given by Britain to Spain 1783

St Marys

FLORIDA

Gulf   of   Mexico

0   300

Miles

/// Spanish possessions
••• United States demand 1779
– – – French proposal for western boundary of U.S. August 1782
≡≡≡ French proposal for Indian country to be under U.S. protection 1782
–•–•– Spanish proposal for western boundary of U.S. 1782
▬▬▬ British proposal adopted as final line in Treaty of Paris 1783

26

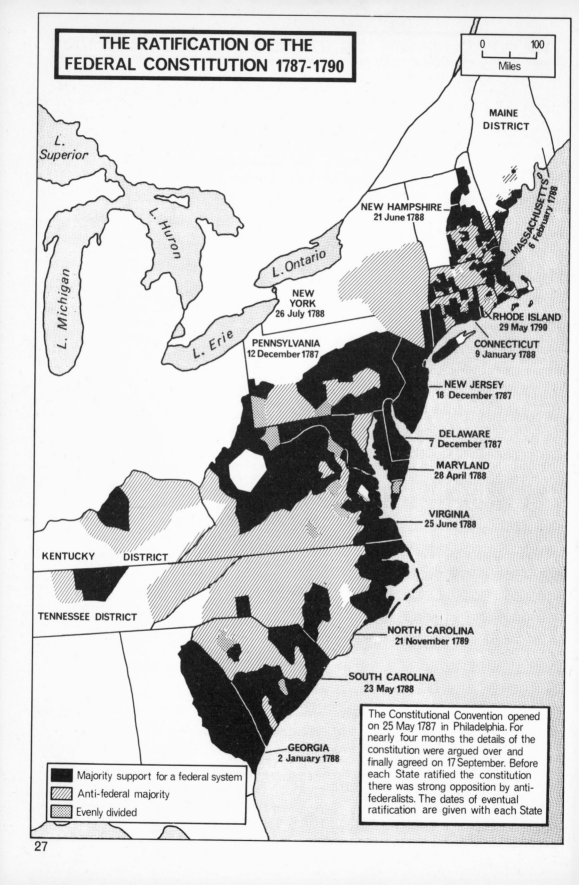

THE RATIFICATION OF THE FEDERAL CONSTITUTION 1787-1790

0   100
Miles

MAINE
DISTRICT

L. Superior

L. Huron

L. Michigan

L. Ontario

L. Erie

NEW HAMPSHIRE
21 June 1788

MASSACHUSETTS
6 February 1788

NEW
YORK
26 July 1788

RHODE ISLAND
29 May 1790

PENNSYLVANIA
12 December 1787

CONNECTICUT
9 January 1788

NEW JERSEY
18 December 1787

DELAWARE
7 December 1787

MARYLAND
28 April 1788

VIRGINIA
25 June 1788

KENTUCKY   DISTRICT

TENNESSEE DISTRICT

NORTH CAROLINA
21 November 1789

SOUTH CAROLINA
23 May 1788

GEORGIA
2 January 1788

■ Majority support for a federal system
▨ Anti-federal majority
▤ Evenly divided

The Constitutional Convention opened
on 25 May 1787 in Philadelphia. For
nearly four months the details of the
constitution were argued over and
finally agreed on 17 September. Before
each State ratified the constitution
there was strong opposition by anti-
federalists. The dates of eventual
ratification are given with each State

27

NORTH AMERICA 1783

Legend:
- The United States of America.
- British claims not finally ceded to U.S. until the Jay Treaty of 1795.
- British possessions.
- Spanish possessions.
- Disputed and unsettled frontiers

ALASKA

Kodiak

1784 Russian settlement founded

UNEXPLORED TERRITORY

BAFFIN LAND

HUDSON BAY

NEW BRITAIN

LABRADOR

NEWFOUNDLAND

NEW SOUTH WALES

CANADA

ACADIA

NOVA SCOTIA

Northern limit of Spanish claims

Columbia

Snake

CALIFORNIA

Mississippi

THE UNITED STATES

Rio Grande

TEXAS

FLORIDA

BAHAMAS

MEXICO

CUBA

JAMAICA

BELIZE

MOSQUITO COAST

PANAMA

0   1000

Miles

By the Treaty of Paris, 3 September 1783, Britain recognised the independence of the United States, withdrew all military and naval forces, agreed to fix the boundary of Canada by negotiation and returned Florida to Spain.

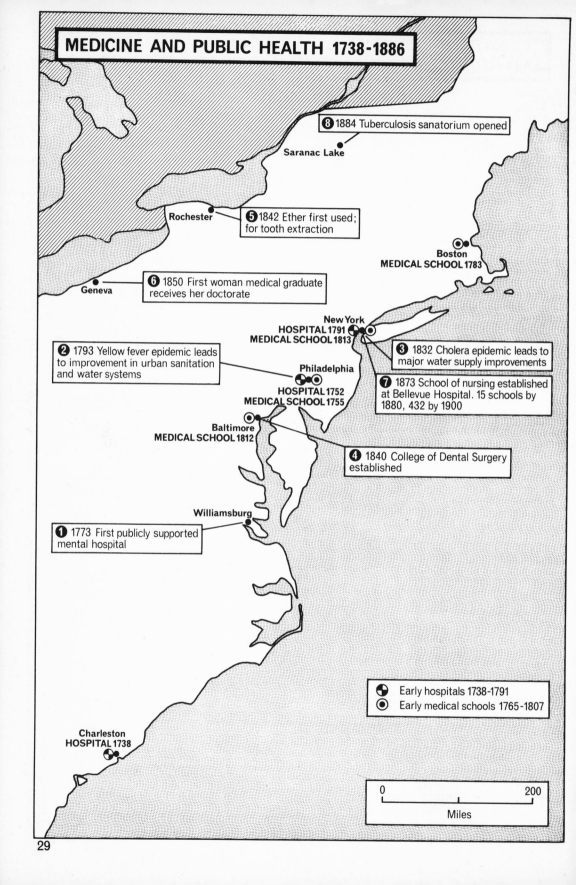

MEDICINE AND PUBLIC HEALTH 1738-1886

8 1884 Tuberculosis sanatorium opened

Saranac Lake

Rochester

5 1842 Ether first used; for tooth extraction

Boston
MEDICAL SCHOOL 1783

6 1850 First woman medical graduate receives her doctorate

Geneva

New York
HOSPITAL 1791
MEDICAL SCHOOL 1813

2 1793 Yellow fever epidemic leads to improvement in urban sanitation and water systems

3 1832 Cholera epidemic leads to major water supply improvements

Philadelphia
HOSPITAL 1752
MEDICAL SCHOOL 1755

7 1873 School of nursing established at Bellevue Hospital. 15 schools by 1880, 432 by 1900

Baltimore
MEDICAL SCHOOL 1812

4 1840 College of Dental Surgery established

Williamsburg

1 1773 First publicly supported mental hospital

⊕ Early hospitals 1738-1791
◉ Early medical schools 1765-1807

Charleston
HOSPITAL 1738

0   200
Miles

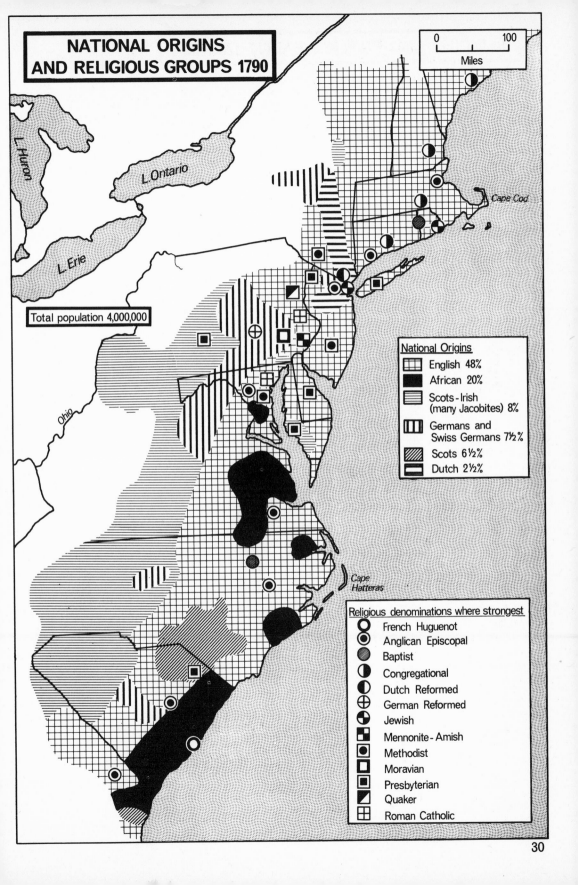

NATIONAL ORIGINS AND RELIGIOUS GROUPS 1790

0   100
Miles

L. Huron

L. Ontario

L. Erie

Cape Cod

Total population 4,000,000

Ohio

Cape Hatteras

National Origins
	English 48%	
	African 20%	
	Scots-Irish (many Jacobites) 8%	
	Germans and Swiss Germans 7½%	
	Scots 6½%	
	Dutch 2½%	

Religious denominations where strongest
	French Huguenot
	Anglican Episcopal
	Baptist
	Congregational
	Dutch Reformed
	German Reformed
	Jewish
	Mennonite - Amish
	Methodist
	Moravian
	Presbyterian
	Quaker
	Roman Catholic

30

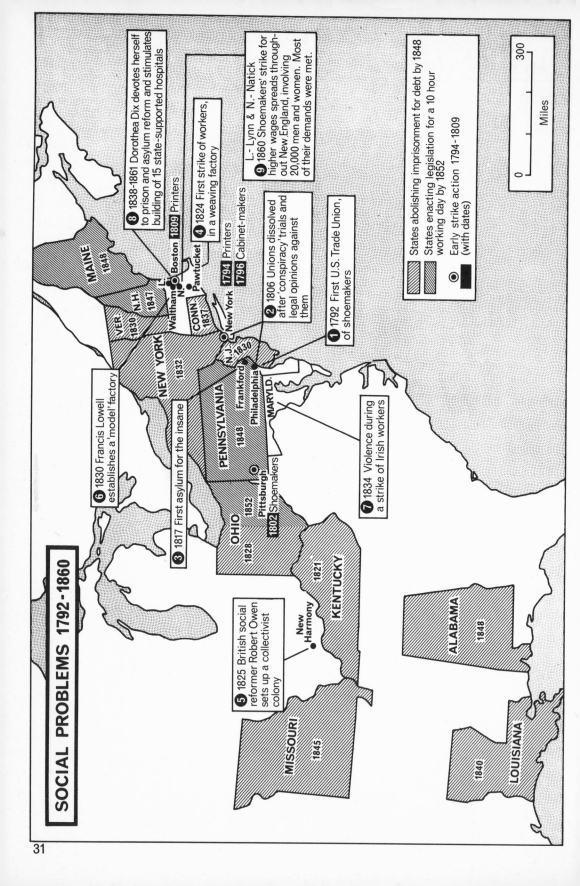

SOCIAL PROBLEMS 1792-1860

8 1838-1861 Dorothea Dix devotes herself to prison and asylum reform and stimulates building of 15 state-supported hospitals

Boston **1809** Printers

4 1824 First strike of workers, in a weaving factory

L- Lynn & N- Natick

9 1860 Shoemakers' strike for higher wages spreads throughout New.England, involving 20,000 men and women. Most of their demands were met.

1794 Printers
1796 Cabinet-makers

2 1806 Unions dissolved after 'conspiracy' trials and legal opinions against them

1 1792 First U.S. Trade Union, of shoemakers

MAINE 1848

N.H. 1847

VER 1830

Waltham
N

CONN 1837

New York

Pawtucket

MARYLD

6 1830 Francis Lowell establishes a 'model' factory

NEW YORK 1832

N.J. 1830

3 1817 First asylum for the insane

PENNSYLVANIA
1848
Frankford
Philadelphia

7 1834 Violence during a strike of Irish workers

OHIO
1828
1852 Pittsburgh
1802 Shoemakers

KENTUCKY
1821

5 1825 British social reformer Robert Owen sets up a collectivist colony

New Harmony

MISSOURI
1845

ALABAMA
1848

LOUISIANA
1840

States abolishing imprisonment for debt by 1848

States enacting legislation for a 10 hour working day by 1852

Early strike action 1794-1809 (with dates)

0   300
Miles

31

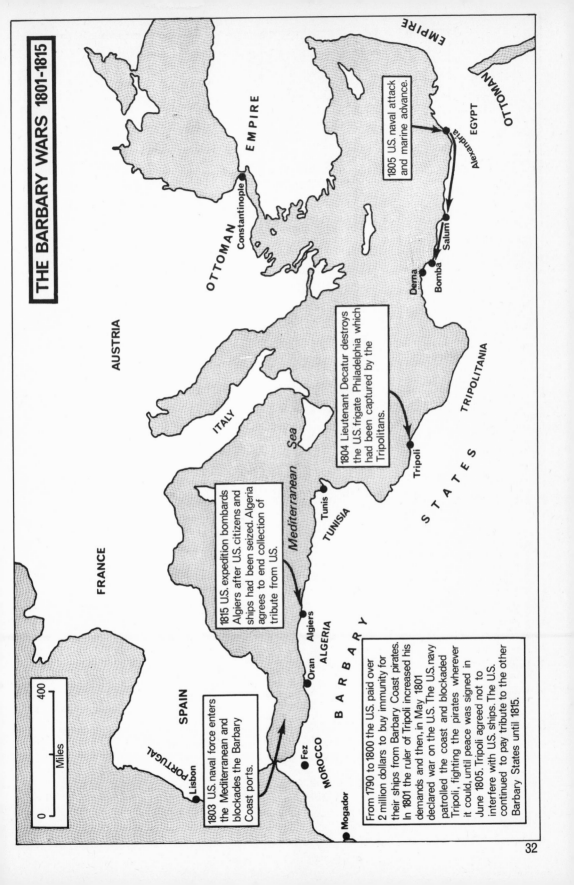

THE BARBARY WARS 1801-1815

OTTOMAN EMPIRE

OTTOMAN EMPIRE

Constantinople

AUSTRIA

FRANCE

ITALY

SPAIN

PORTUGAL

Lisbon

Mediterranean Sea

MOROCCO

Fez

Mogador

Oran

Algiers

ALGERIA

B A R B A R Y

Tunis

TUNISIA

Tripoli

S T A T E S

TRIPOLITANIA

Derna

Bomba

Salum

Alexandria

EGYPT

OTTOMAN

1805 U.S. naval attack and marine advance.

1804 Lieutenant Decatur destroys the U.S. frigate Philadelphia which had been captured by the Tripolitans.

1815 U.S. expedition bombards Algiers after U.S. citizens and ships had been seized. Algeria agrees to end collection of tribute from U.S.

1803 U.S. naval force enters the Mediterranean and blockades the Barbary Coast ports.

From 1790 to 1800 the U.S. paid over 2 million dollars to buy immunity for their ships from Barbary Coast pirates. In 1801 the ruler of Tripoli increased his demands and then, in May 1801 declared war on the U.S. The U.S. navy patrolled the coast and blockaded Tripoli, fighting the pirates wherever it could, until peace was signed in June 1805. Tripoli agreed not to interfere with U.S. ships. The U.S. continued to pay tribute to the other Barbary States until 1815.

0 400 Miles

32

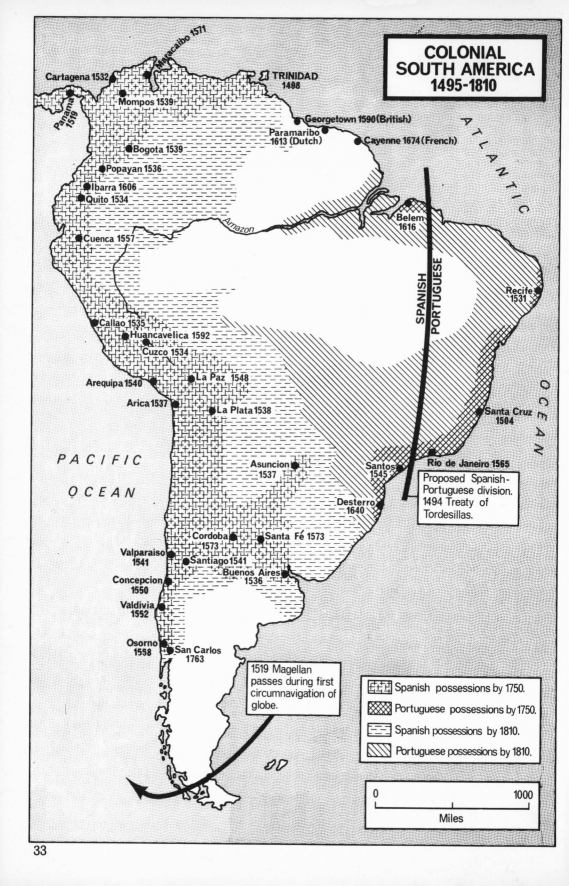

COLONIAL SOUTH AMERICA 1495-1810

Cartagena 1532

Maracaibo 1571

Panama 1519

Mompos 1539

TRINIDAD 1498

Georgetown 1590 (British)

Paramaribo 1613 (Dutch)

Cayenne 1674 (French)

Bogota 1539

Popayan 1536

Ibarra 1606

Quito 1534

Cuenca 1557

Amazon

Belem 1616

SPANISH

PORTUGESE

Recife 1531

Callao 1535

Huancavelica 1592

Cuzco 1534

Arequipa 1540

La Paz 1548

Arica 1537

La Plata 1538

Santa Cruz 1504

PACIFIC

OCEAN

Asuncion 1537

Santos 1545

Rio de Janeiro 1565

Desterro 1640

Proposed Spanish-Portuguese division. 1494 Treaty of Tordesillas.

Cordoba 1573

Santa Fé 1573

Valparaiso 1541

Santiago 1541

Buenos Aires 1536

Concepcion 1550

Valdivia 1552

Osorno 1558

San Carlos 1763

1519 Magellan passes during first circumnavigation of globe.

ATLANTIC

OCEAN

Spanish possessions by 1750.

Portuguese possessions by 1750.

Spanish possessions by 1810.

Portuguese possessions by 1810.

0   1000

Miles

33

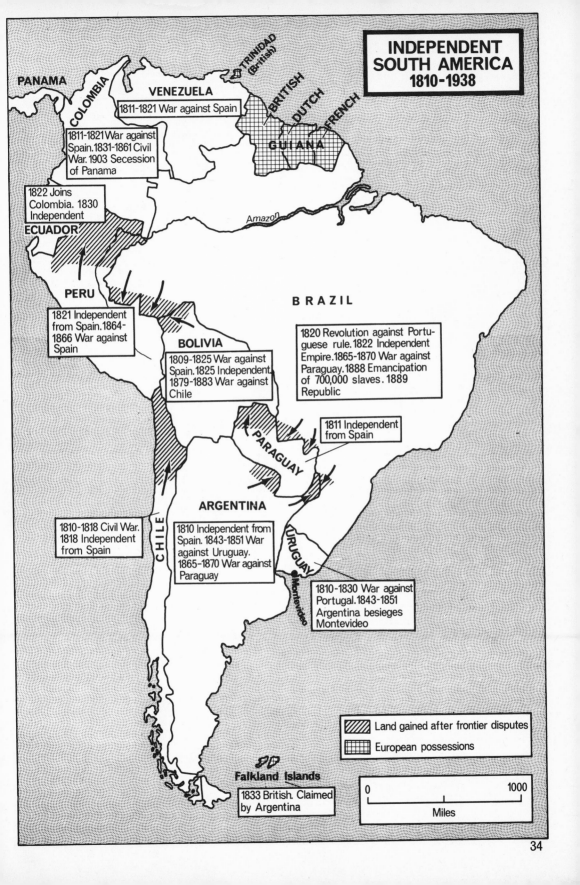

INDEPENDENT SOUTH AMERICA 1810-1938

PANAMA

COLOMBIA

VENEZUELA

1811-1821 War against Spain

1811-1821 War against Spain. 1831-1861 Civil War. 1903 Secession of Panama

TRINIDAD (British)

BRITISH DUTCH FRENCH

GUIANA

1822 Joins Colombia. 1830 Independent

ECUADOR

Amazon

PERU

1821 Independent from Spain. 1864-1866 War against Spain

BRAZIL

BOLIVIA

1809-1825 War against Spain. 1825 Independent. 1879-1883 War against Chile

1820 Revolution against Portuguese rule. 1822 Independent Empire. 1865-1870 War against Paraguay. 1888 Emancipation of 700,000 slaves. 1889 Republic

PARAGUAY

1811 Independent from Spain

ARGENTINA

1810-1818 Civil War. 1818 Independent from Spain

CHILE

1810 Independent from Spain. 1843-1851 War against Uruguay. 1865-1870 War against Paraguay

URUGUAY

Montevideo

1810-1830 War against Portugal. 1843-1851 Argentina besieges Montevideo

Falkland Islands

1833 British. Claimed by Argentina

///// Land gained after frontier disputes

▦ European possessions

0 ———————— 1000

Miles

34

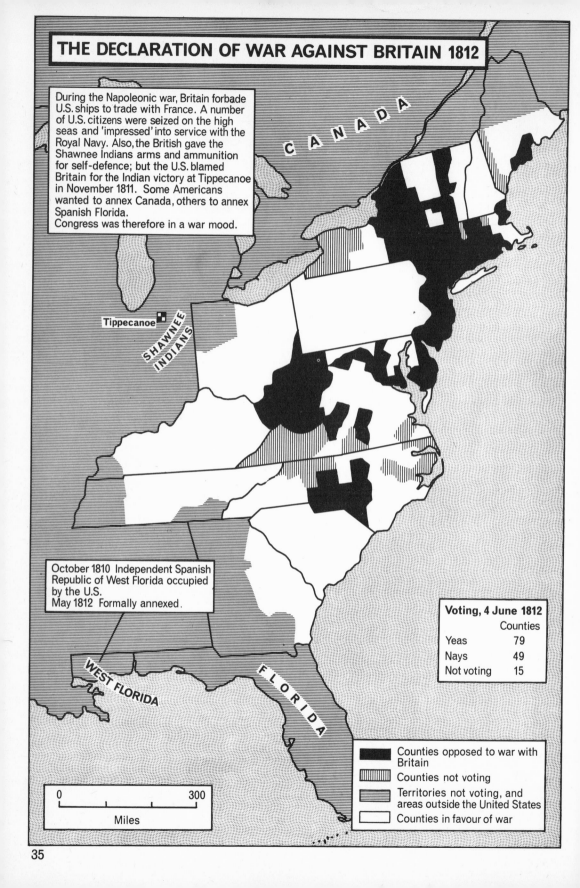

THE DECLARATION OF WAR AGAINST BRITAIN 1812

During the Napoleonic war, Britain forbade U.S. ships to trade with France. A number of U.S. citizens were seized on the high seas and 'impressed' into service with the Royal Navy. Also, the British gave the Shawnee Indians arms and ammunition for self-defence; but the U.S. blamed Britain for the Indian victory at Tippecanoe in November 1811. Some Americans wanted to annex Canada, others to annex Spanish Florida.
Congress was therefore in a war mood.

CANADA

Tippecanoe

SHAWNEE INDIANS

October 1810 Independent Spanish Republic of West Florida occupied by the U.S.
May 1812 Formally annexed.

WEST FLORIDA

FLORIDA

Voting, 4 June 1812

	Counties
Yeas	79
Nays	49
Not voting	15

Counties opposed to war with Britain

Counties not voting

Territories not voting, and areas outside the United States

Counties in favour of war

0   300

Miles

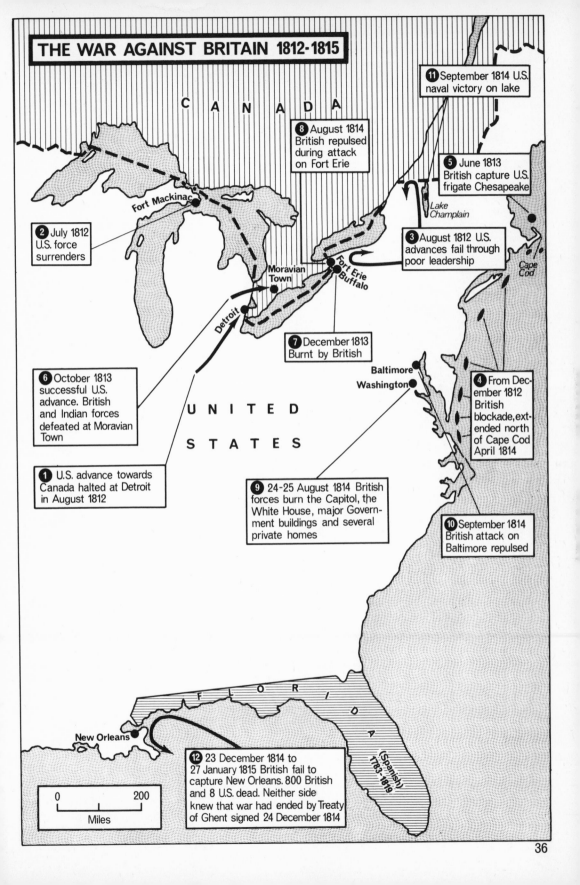

THE WAR AGAINST BRITAIN 1812-1815

C A N A D A

11 September 1814 U.S. naval victory on lake

8 August 1814 British repulsed during attack on Fort Erie

5 June 1813 British capture U.S. frigate Chesapeake

Lake Champlain

2 July 1812 U.S. force surrenders

Fort Mackinac

3 August 1812 U.S. advances fail through poor leadership

Cape Cod

Moravian Town

Fort Erie
Buffalo

Detroit

7 December 1813 Burnt by British

6 October 1813 successful U.S. advance. British and Indian forces defeated at Moravian Town

Baltimore
Washington

U N I T E D

S T A T E S

4 From December 1812 British blockade, extended north of Cape Cod April 1814

1 U.S. advance towards Canada halted at Detroit in August 1812

9 24-25 August 1814 British forces burn the Capitol, the White House, major Government buildings and several private homes

10 September 1814 British attack on Baltimore repulsed

F L O R I D A

New Orleans

12 23 December 1814 to 27 January 1815 British fail to capture New Orleans. 800 British and 8 U.S. dead. Neither side knew that war had ended by Treaty of Ghent signed 24 December 1814

(Spanish) 1783-1819

0   200
Miles

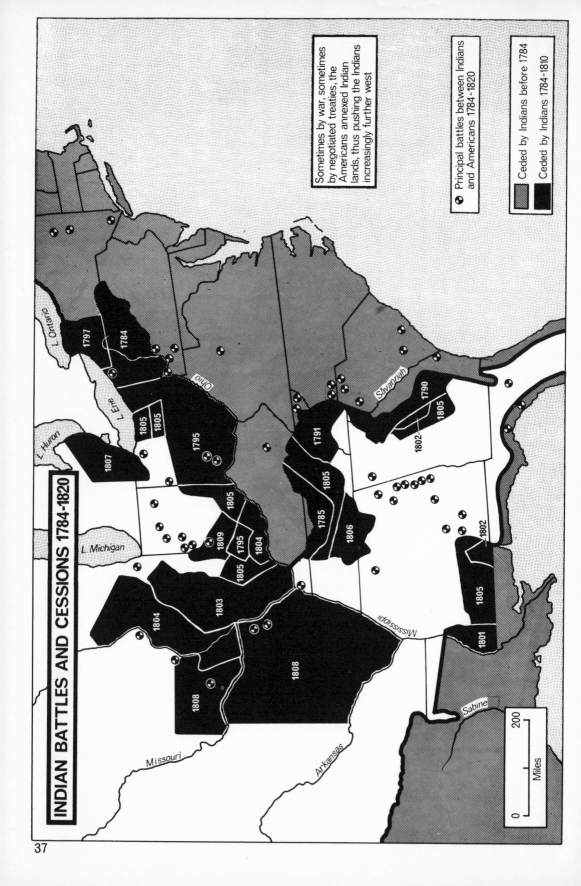

INDIAN BATTLES AND CESSIONS 1784-1820

Sometimes by war, sometimes by negotiated treaties, the Americans annexed Indian lands, thus pushing the Indians increasingly further west

⊕ Principal battles between Indians and Americans 1784-1820

Ceded by Indians before 1784

Ceded by Indians 1784-1810

L. Ontario

L. Erie

L. Huron

L. Michigan

Ohio

Savannah

Mississippi

Missouri

Arkansas

Sabine

1797
1784
1805
1805
1807
1795
1805
1805
1809
1795
1804
1805
1803
1804
1808
1791
1805
1785
1806
1790
1805
1802
1802
1805
1801

200

Miles

0

37

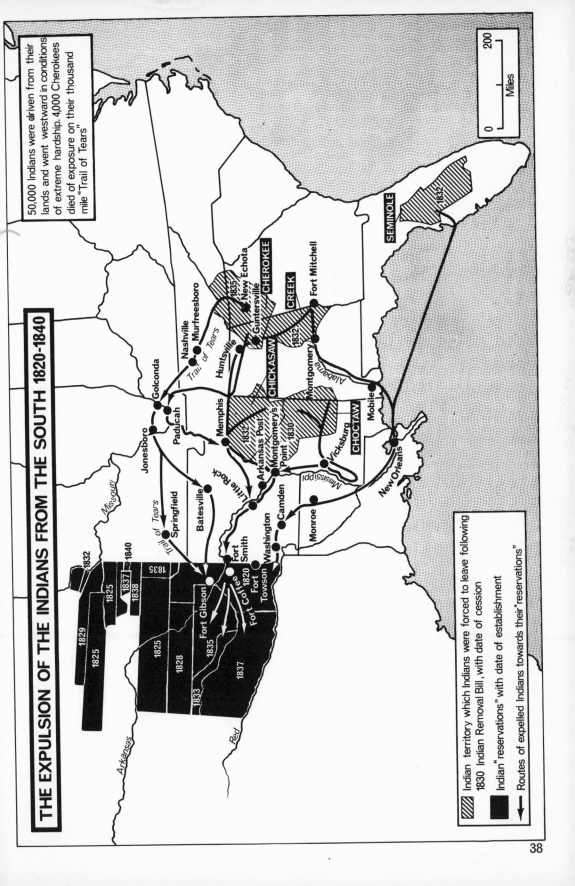

THE EXPULSION OF THE INDIANS FROM THE SOUTH 1820-1840

50,000 Indians were driven from their lands and went westward in conditions of extreme hardship. 4,000 Cherokees died of exposure on their thousand mile "Trail of Tears"

200

0

Miles

Nashville
Murfreesboro
New Echota
1835
Guntersville
CHEROKEE
Huntsville
CREEK
CHICKASAW
1832
Fort Mitchell
Montgomery
Alabama

Golconda
Paducah
Memphis
Trail of Tears
1832
Arkansas Post
Montgomery's
Point
1830
Mobile
CHOCTAW
Vicksburg
Mississippi
New Orleans

Jonesboro
Missouri
Springfield
Trail of Tears
Batesville
Little Rock
Camden
Monroe

Arkansas
1832
1840
1825
1837
1838
1835
Fort
Smith
Washington
Fort
Coffee 1820
Fort Gibson
Fort
Towson

1829
1825
1825
1828
1835
1837
1833
Red

☐ Indian territory which Indians were forced to leave following 1830 Indian Removal Bill, with date of cession

■ Indian "reservations" with date of establishment

→ Routes of expelled Indians towards their "reservations"

SEMINOLE
1835

38

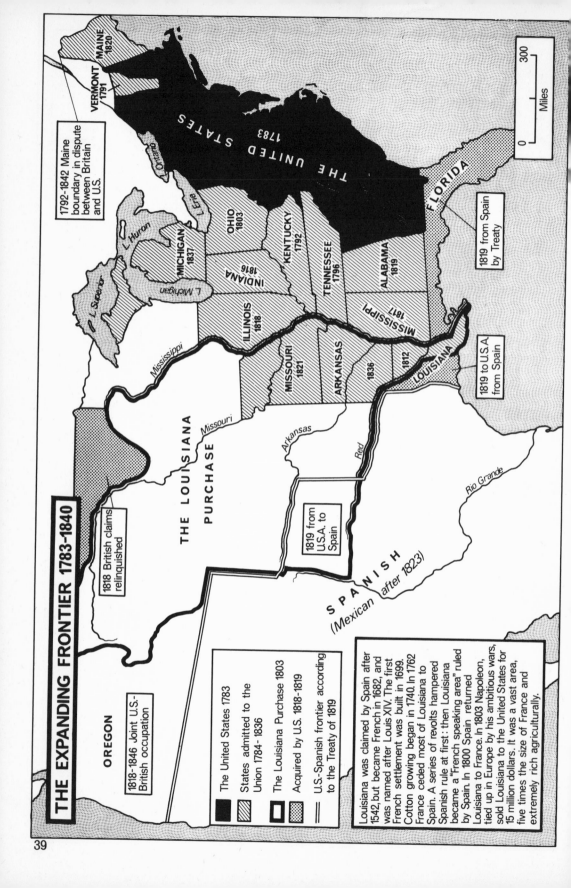

THE EXPANDING FRONTIER 1783-1840

THE UNITED STATES 1783

MAINE 1820

VERMONT 1791

1792-1842 Maine boundary in dispute between Britain and U.S.

L. Ontario

L. Erie

L. Huron

L. Michigan

L. Superior

MICHIGAN 1837

OHIO 1803

INDIANA 1816

KENTUCKY 1792

TENNESSEE 1796

ALABAMA 1819

MISSISSIPPI 1817

ILLINOIS 1818

MISSOURI 1821

ARKANSAS 1836

1836

1812

LOUISIANA

FLORIDA

1819 from Spain by Treaty

1819 to U.S.A. from Spain

Mississippi

Missouri

Arkansas

Red

Rio Grande

THE LOUISIANA PURCHASE

1819 from U.S.A. to Spain

SPANISH
(Mexican after 1823)

1818 British claims relinquished

OREGON

1818-1846 Joint U.S.-British occupation

0 300 Miles

The United States 1783

States admitted to the Union 1784- 1836

The Louisiana Purchase 1803

Acquired by U.S. 1818-1819

U.S.-Spanish frontier according to the Treaty of 1819

Louisiana was claimed by Spain after 1542, but became French in 1682, and was named after Louis XIV. The first French settlement was built in 1699. Cotton growing began in 1740. In 1762 France ceded most of Louisiana to Spain. A series of revolts hampered Spanish rule at first: then Louisiana became a "French speaking area" ruled by Spain. In 1800 Spain returned Louisiana to France. In 1803 Napoleon, tied up in Europe by his ambitious wars, sold Louisiana to the United States for 15 million dollars. It was a vast area, five times the size of France and extremely rich agriculturally.

39

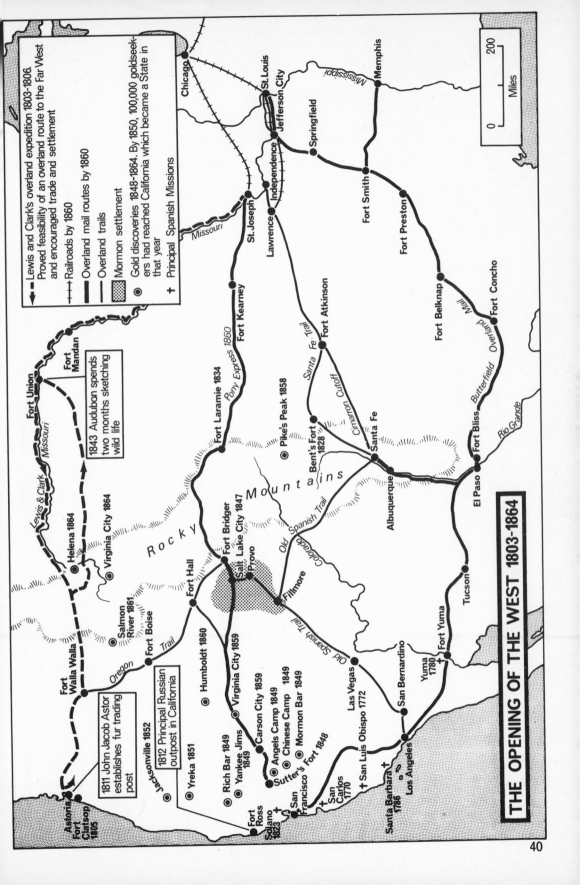

THE OPENING OF THE WEST 1803-1864

Legend:
- ◄─ ─► Lewis and Clark's overland expedition 1803-1806. Proved feasibility of an overland route to the Far West and encouraged trade and settlement
- ┼┼┼┼ Railroads by 1860
- ▬▬▬ Overland mail routes by 1860
- ▬▬▬ Overland trails
- ░░░ Mormon settlement
- ⊙ Gold discoveries 1848-1864. By 1850, 100,000 goldseekers had reached California which became a State in that year
- ✝ Principal Spanish Missions

1811 John Jacob Astor establishes fur trading post

1812 Principal Russian outpost in California

1843 Audubon spends two months sketching wild life

200

0   Miles

Memphis

Chicago

St. Louis

Jefferson City

Springfield

Independence

Lawrence

St. Joseph

Fort Smith

Fort Preston

Fort Concho

Mississippi

Missouri

Fort Kearney

Fort Atkinson

Fort Belknap

Fort Laramie 1834

Pony Express 1860

Pike's Peak 1858

Bent's Fort 1828

Santa Fe Trail

Cimarron Cutoff

Santa Fe

Fort Bliss

El Paso

Albuquerque

Rio Grande

Butterfield

Overland Mail

Fort Mandan

Fort Union

Lewis & Clark

Missouri

Helena 1864

Virginia City 1864

Salmon River 1861

Fort Boise

Oregon Trail

Fort Walla Walla

Astoria Fort Clatsop 1805

Fort Ross

Jacksonville 1852

Yreka 1851

Rich Bar 1849

Yankee Jims 1849

Carson City 1859

Virginia City 1859

Humboldt 1860

Angels Camp 1849

Chinese Camp 1849

Mormon Bar 1849

Sutter's Fort 1848

San Francisco

Solano 1823

Rocky   Mountains

Fort Hall

Fort Bridger

Salt Lake City 1847

Provo

Fillmore

Old Spanish Trail

Colorado

Las Vegas

San Bernardino

San Luis Obispo 1772

San Carlos 1770

Santa Barbara 1786

Los Angeles

Fort Yuma

Yuma 1780

Tucson

Old Spanish Trail

40

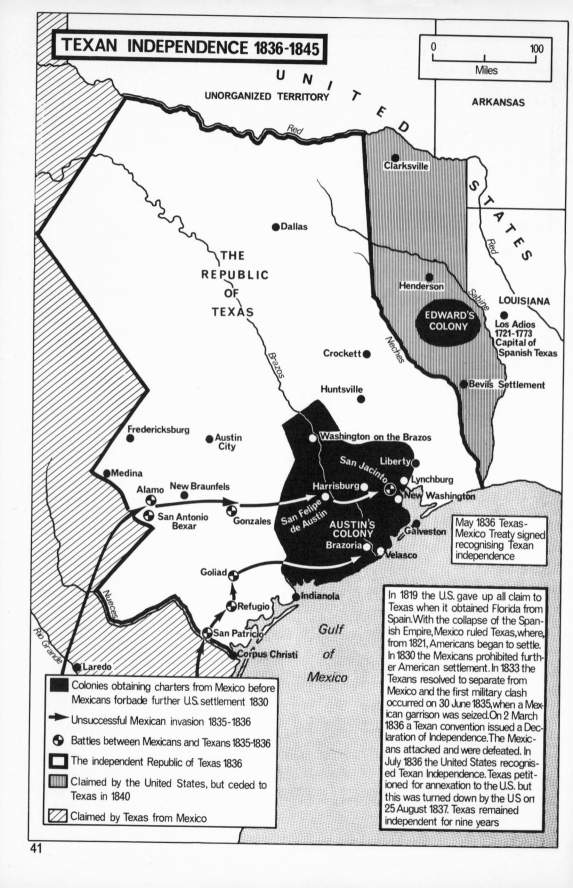

TEXAN INDEPENDENCE 1836-1845

0   100

Miles

U N I T E D

UNORGANIZED TERRITORY

ARKANSAS

S T A T E S

Red

Clarksville

LOUISIANA

Dallas

THE
REPUBLIC
OF
TEXAS

Henderson

EDWARD'S
COLONY

Los Adios
1721-1773
Capital of
Spanish Texas

Crockett

Bevil's Settlement

Huntsville

Fredericksburg

Austin
City

Washington on the Brazos

Liberty

San Jacinto

Lynchburg

Medina

Harrisburg

New Washington

Alamo

New Braunfels

San Antonio
Bexar

Gonzales

San Felipe
de Austin

AUSTIN'S
COLONY

Galveston

May 1836 Texas-
Mexico Treaty signed
recognising Texan
independence

Brazoria

Velasco

Goliad

Indianola

Gulf

Refugio

of

San Patricio

Mexico

Corpus Christi

Laredo

Rio Grande

Nueces

Brazos

Neches

Sabine

Red

In 1819 the U.S. gave up all claim to
Texas when it obtained Florida from
Spain. With the collapse of the Spanish Empire, Mexico ruled Texas, where,
from 1821, Americans began to settle.
In 1830 the Mexicans prohibited further American settlement. In 1833 the
Texans resolved to separate from
Mexico and the first military clash
occurred on 30 June 1835, when a Mexican garrison was seized. On 2 March
1836 a Texan convention issued a Declaration of Independence. The Mexicans attacked and were defeated. In
July 1836 the United States recognised Texan Independence. Texas petit-
ioned for annexation to the U.S. but
this was turned down by the US on
25 August 1837. Texas remained
independent for nine years

◼ Colonies obtaining charters from Mexico before
Mexicans forbade further U.S. settlement 1830

→ Unsuccessful Mexican invasion 1835-1836

✚ Battles between Mexicans and Texans 1835-1836

☐ The independent Republic of Texas 1836

▥ Claimed by the United States, but ceded to
Texas in 1840

▨ Claimed by Texas from Mexico

41

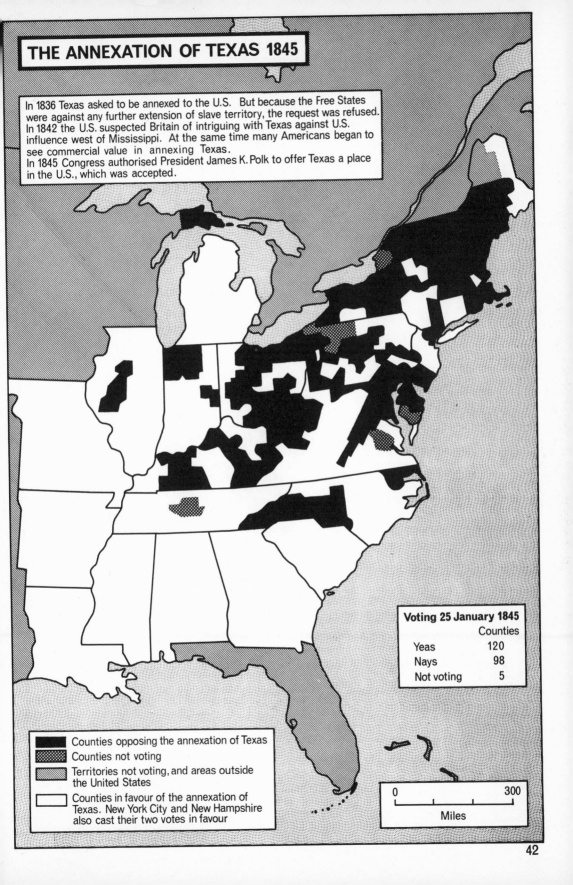

THE ANNEXATION OF TEXAS 1845

In 1836 Texas asked to be annexed to the U.S. But because the Free States were against any further extension of slave territory, the request was refused. In 1842 the U.S. suspected Britain of intriguing with Texas against U.S. influence west of Mississippi. At the same time many Americans began to see commercial value in annexing Texas.
In 1845 Congress authorised President James K. Polk to offer Texas a place in the U.S., which was accepted.

Voting 25 January 1845

	Counties
Yeas	120
Nays	98
Not voting	5

Counties opposing the annexation of Texas

Counties not voting

Territories not voting, and areas outside the United States

Counties in favour of the annexation of Texas. New York City and New Hampshire also cast their two votes in favour

0 — 300
Miles

42

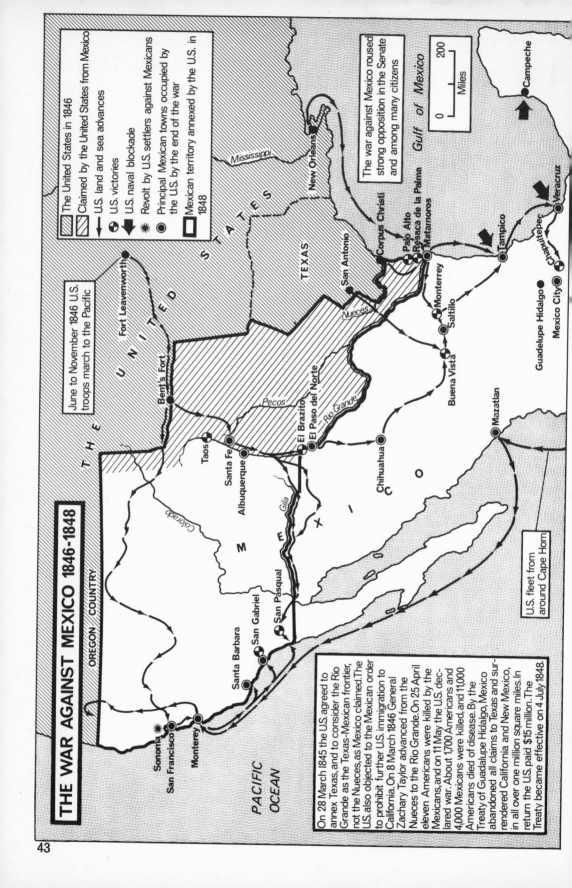

THE WAR AGAINST MEXICO 1846-1848

Legend:

- The United States in 1846
- Claimed by the United States from Mexico
- U.S. land and sea advances
- U.S. victories
- U.S. naval blockade
- Revolt by U.S. settlers against Mexicans
- Principal Mexican towns occupied by the U.S. by the end of the war
- Mexican territory annexed by the U.S. in 1848

June to November 1846 U.S. troops march to the Pacific

The war against Mexico roused strong opposition in the Senate and among many citizens

0   200
Miles

U.S. fleet from around Cape Horn

On 28 March 1845 the U.S. agreed to annex Texas, and to consider the Rio Grande as the Texas-Mexico frontier, not the Nueces, as Mexico claimed. The U.S. also objected to the Mexican order to prohibit further U.S. immigration to California. On 8 March 1846 General Zachary Taylor advanced from the Nueces to the Rio Grande. On 25 April eleven Americans were killed by the Mexicans, and on 11 May the U.S. declared war. About 1,700 Americans and 4,000 Mexicans were killed, and 11,000 Americans died of disease. By the Treaty of Guadalupe Hidalgo, Mexico abandoned all claims to Texas and surrendered California and New Mexico, in all over one million square miles. In return the U.S. paid $15 million. The Treaty became effective on 4 July 1848.

Place names and features:

OREGON COUNTRY

THE UNITED STATES

TEXAS

M E X I C O

PACIFIC OCEAN

Gulf of Mexico

Mississippi
Pecos
Rio Grande
Nueces
Colorado
Gila

Fort Leavenworth
Bent's Fort
New Orleans
San Antonio
Corpus Christi
Palo Alto
Resaca de la Palma
Matamoros
Taos
Santa Fe
Albuquerque
El Brazito
El Paso del Norte
Chihuahua
Monterrey
Saltillo
Buena Vista
Tampico
Chapultepec
Veracruz
Campeche
Guadalupe Hidalgo
Mexico City
Mazatlan
Sonoma
San Francisco
Monterey
Santa Barbara
San Gabriel
San Pasqual

43

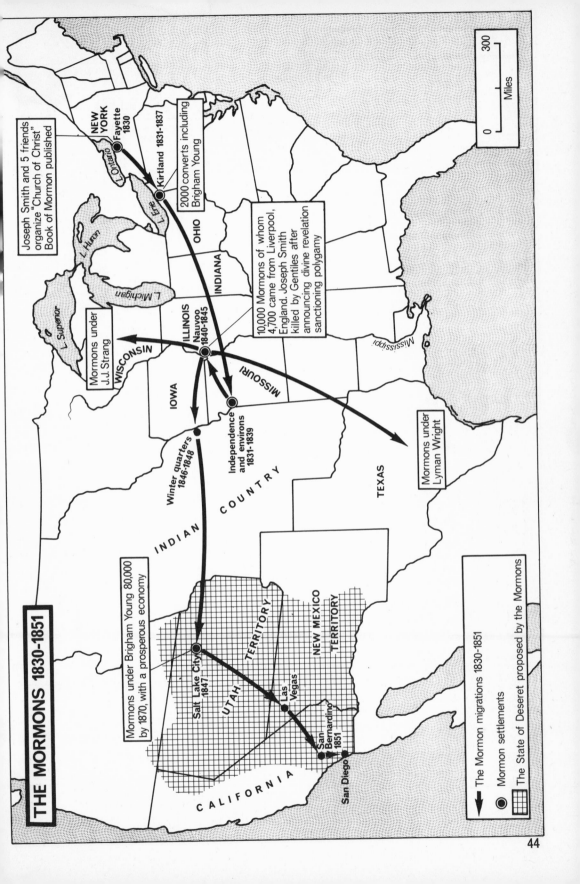

THE MORMONS 1830-1851

Joseph Smith and 5 friends organize "Church of Christ" Book of Mormon published

NEW YORK
Fayette 1830

L. Ontario

L. Erie

Kirtland 1831-1837

2000 converts including Brigham Young

OHIO

L. Huron

L. Michigan

L. Superior

INDIANA

10,000 Mormons of whom 4,700 came from Liverpool, England. Joseph Smith killed by Gentiles after announcing divine revelation sanctioning polygamy

Mormons under J.J. Strang

WISCONSIN

ILLINOIS
Nauvoo 1840-1845

Mississippi

IOWA

Winter quarters 1846-1848

Independence and environs 1831-1839

MISSOURI

INDIAN COUNTRY

TEXAS

Mormons under Lyman Wright

Mormons under Brigham Young 80,000 by 1870, with a prosperous economy

UTAH TERRITORY

Salt Lake City 1847

Las Vegas

NEW MEXICO TERRITORY

San Bernardino 1851

San Diego

CALIFORNIA

300

0

Miles

The Mormon migrations 1830-1851

Mormon settlements

The State of Deseret proposed by the Mormons

44

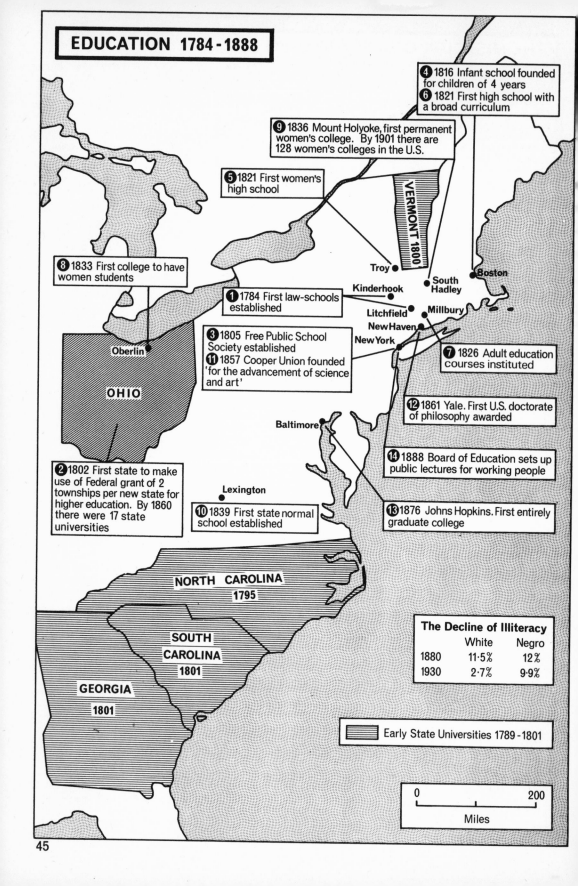

EDUCATION 1784-1888

4 1816 Infant school founded for children of 4 years

6 1821 First high school with a broad curriculum

9 1836 Mount Holyoke, first permanent women's college. By 1901 there are 128 women's colleges in the U.S.

5 1821 First women's high school

VERMONT 1800

8 1833 First college to have women students

1 1784 First law-schools established

Troy

Kinderhook

South Hadley

Boston

3 1805 Free Public School Society established

11 1857 Cooper Union founded 'for the advancement of science and art'

Litchfield

Millbury

New Haven

New York

Oberlin

OHIO

7 1826 Adult education courses instituted

12 1861 Yale. First U.S. doctorate of philosophy awarded

Baltimore

14 1888 Board of Education sets up public lectures for working people

2 1802 First state to make use of Federal grant of 2 townships per new state for higher education. By 1860 there were 17 state universities

Lexington

10 1839 First state normal school established

13 1876 Johns Hopkins. First entirely graduate college

NORTH CAROLINA
1795

SOUTH CAROLINA
1801

GEORGIA
1801

The Decline of Illiteracy		
	White	Negro
1880	11·5%	12%
1930	2·7%	9·9%

Early State Universities 1789-1801

0   200

Miles

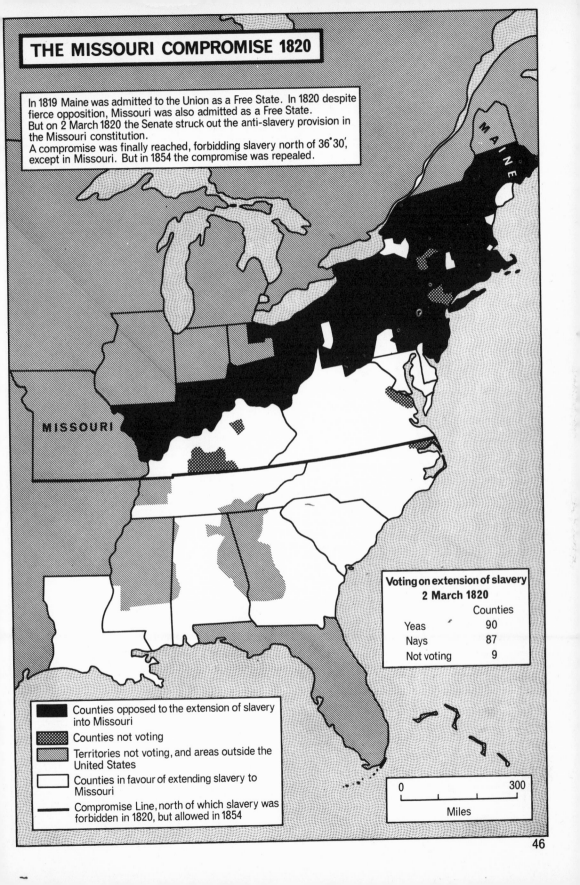

THE MISSOURI COMPROMISE 1820

In 1819 Maine was admitted to the Union as a Free State. In 1820 despite fierce opposition, Missouri was also admitted as a Free State.
But on 2 March 1820 the Senate struck out the anti-slavery provision in the Missouri constitution.
A compromise was finally reached, forbidding slavery north of 36°30', except in Missouri. But in 1854 the compromise was repealed.

MAINE

MISSOURI

Voting on extension of slavery
2 March 1820

	Counties
Yeas	90
Nays	87
Not voting	9

Counties opposed to the extension of slavery into Missouri

Counties not voting

Territories not voting, and areas outside the United States

Counties in favour of extending slavery to Missouri

Compromise Line, north of which slavery was forbidden in 1820, but allowed in 1854

0   300

Miles

46

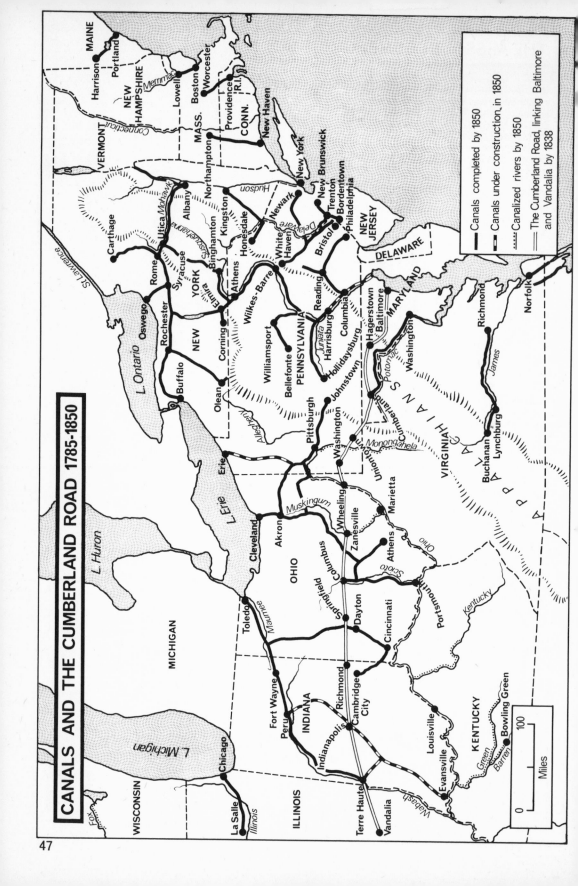

CANALS AND THE CUMBERLAND ROAD 1785-1850

Legend:

━━━ Canals completed by 1850
╌╌╌ Canals under construction, in 1850
┅┅┅ Canalized rivers by 1850
═══ The Cumberland Road, linking Baltimore and Vandalia by 1838

States and regions:
MAINE, NEW HAMPSHIRE, VERMONT, MASS., CONN., R.I., NEW YORK, NEW JERSEY, PENNSYLVANIA, DELAWARE, MARYLAND, VIRGINIA, OHIO, INDIANA, ILLINOIS, WISCONSIN, MICHIGAN, KENTUCKY

Water bodies:
St. Lawrence, L. Ontario, L. Erie, L. Huron, L. Michigan

Rivers:
Merrimac, Connecticut, Hudson, Mohawk, Susquehanna, Delaware, Juniata, Allegheny, Potomac, Cumberland, Monongahela, Muskingum, Scioto, Ohio, Kentucky, Maumee, Wabash, Green, Barren, James, Fox, Illinois

Cities:
Harrison, Portland, Lowell, Worcester, Boston, Providence, New Haven, New York, New Brunswick, Trenton, Bordentown, Newark, Philadelphia, Bristol, White Haven, Athens, Honesdale, Kingston, Northampton, Binghamton, Albany, Utica, Rome, Carthage, Syracuse, Rochester, Oswego, Buffalo, Olean, Corning, Elmira, Wilkes-Barre, Williamsport, Bellefonte, Reading, Columbia, Harrisburg, Hollidaysburg, Johnstown, Pittsburgh, Washington, Hagerstown, Baltimore, Washington, Richmond, Norfolk, Lynchburg, Buchanan, Cleveland, Akron, Wheeling, Zanesville, Marietta, Athens, Columbus, Springfield, Dayton, Cincinnati, Portsmouth, Toledo, Fort Wayne, Peru, Indianapolis, Richmond, Cambridge City, Terre Haute, Vandalia, Evansville, Louisville, Bowling Green, Chicago, La Salle

APPALACHIANS

Miles 0 — 100

47

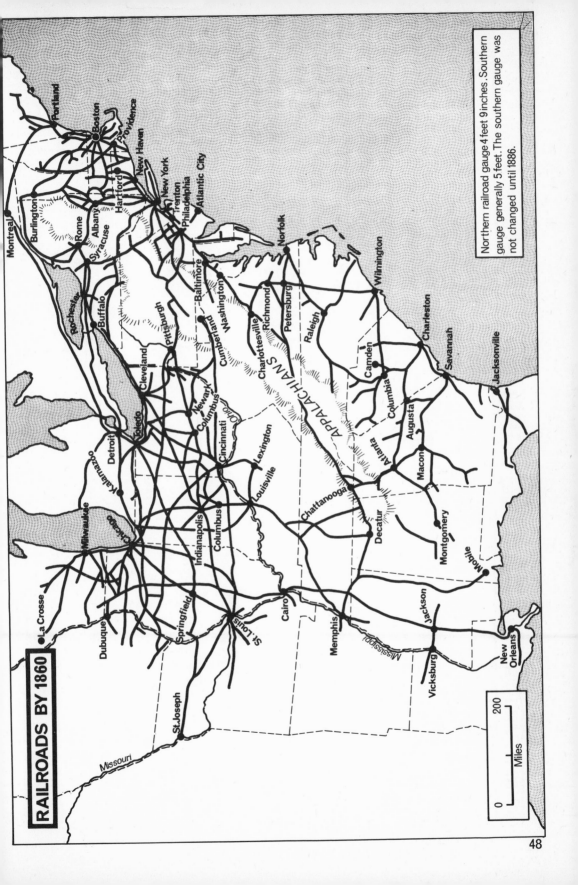

RAILROADS BY 1860

Northern railroad gauge 4 feet 9 inches. Southern gauge generally 5 feet. The southern gauge was not changed until 1886.

0   200

Miles

48

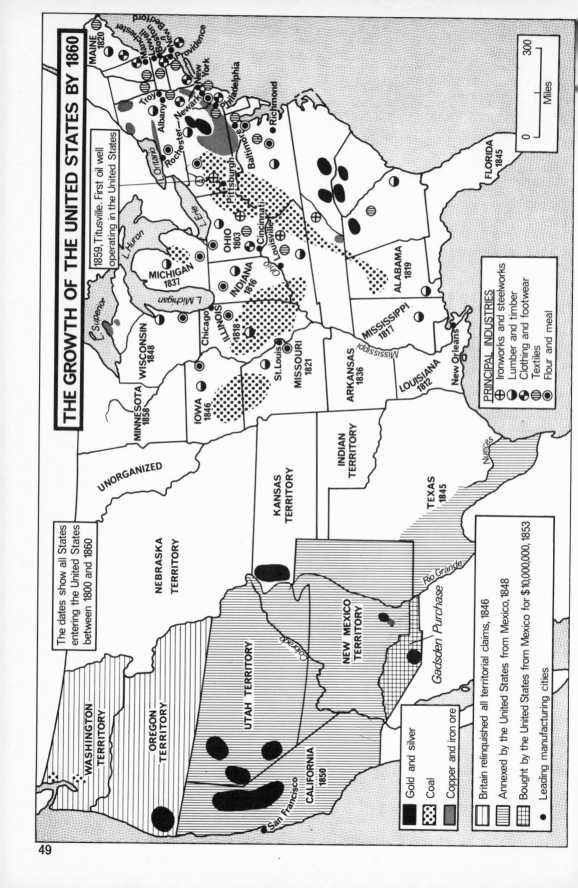

THE GROWTH OF THE UNITED STATES BY 1860

1859, Titusville. First oil well operating in the United States

The dates show all States entering the United States between 1800 and 1860

PRINCIPAL INDUSTRIES
- ⊕ Ironworks and steelworks
- ◑ Lumber and timber
- ● Clothing and footwear
- ◒ Textiles
- ⊜ Flour and meal

Gold and silver
Coal
Copper and iron ore

Britain relinquished all territorial claims, 1846
Annexed by the United States from Mexico, 1848
Bought by the United States from Mexico for $10,000,000, 1853
• Leading manufacturing cities

MAINE 1820
MICHIGAN 1837
WISCONSIN 1848
MINNESOTA 1858
IOWA 1846
ILLINOIS 1818
INDIANA 1816
OHIO 1803
MISSOURI 1821
ARKANSAS 1836
LOUISIANA 1812
MISSISSIPPI 1817
ALABAMA 1819
FLORIDA 1845
TEXAS 1845
CALIFORNIA 1850

UNORGANIZED
NEBRASKA TERRITORY
KANSAS TERRITORY
INDIAN TERRITORY
WASHINGTON TERRITORY
OREGON TERRITORY
UTAH TERRITORY
NEW MEXICO TERRITORY

Gadsden Purchase

Troy
Albany
Rochester
Pittsburgh
Cincinnati
Louisville
Chicago
St. Louis
New Orleans
San Francisco
Boston
Providence
New York
Newark
Philadelphia
Baltimore
Richmond
New Bedford

L. Superior
L. Huron
L. Michigan
L. Ontario
L. Erie
Ohio
Mississippi
Nueces
Rio Grande
Colorado

0   300
Miles

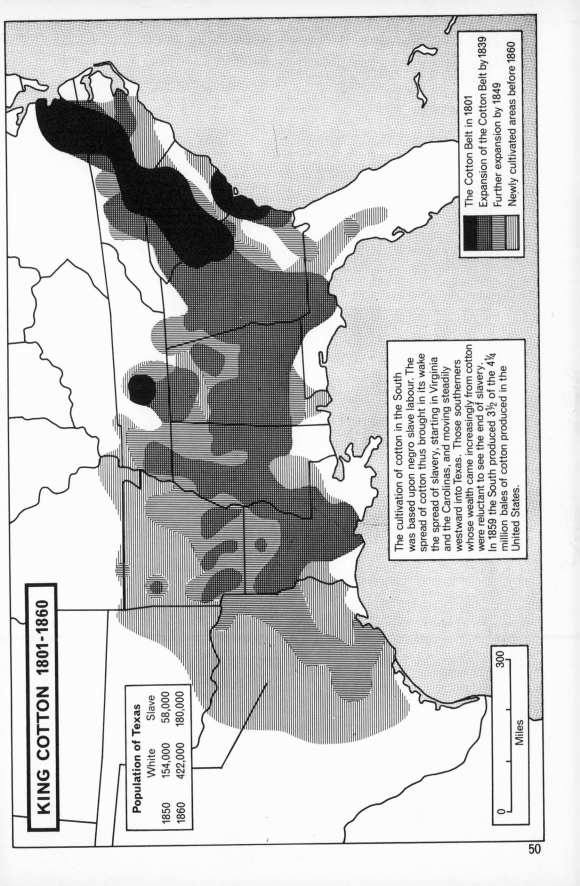

KING COTTON 1801-1860

Population of Texas

	White	Slave
1850	154,000	58,000
1860	422,000	180,000

The cultivation of cotton in the South was based upon negro slave labour. The spread of cotton thus brought in its wake the spread of slavery, starting in Virginia and the Carolinas, and moving steadily westward into Texas. Those southerners whose wealth came increasingly from cotton were reluctant to see the end of slavery. In 1859 the South produced 3½ of the 4¼ million bales of cotton produced in the United States.

The Cotton Belt in 1801
Expansion of the Cotton Belt by 1839
Further expansion by 1849
Newly cultivated areas before 1860

0   300
Miles

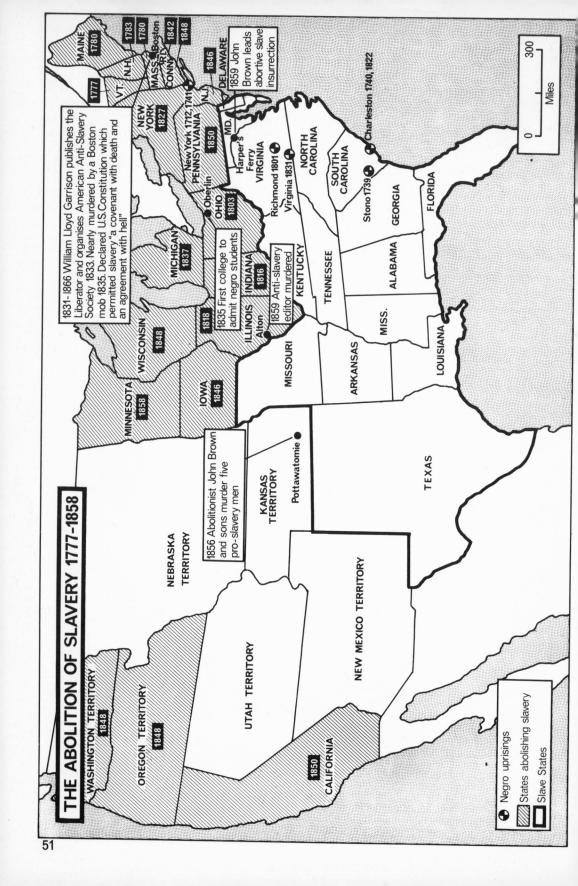

THE ABOLITION OF SLAVERY 1777-1858

MAINE 1780
1783
1780
1842
1848
VT. N.H. 1777
MASS. Boston
R.I. CONN.
N.J.
1846
DELAWARE

1859 John Brown leads abortive slave insurrection

NEW YORK 1827
New York 1712,1741
PENNSYLVANIA 1850
MD.

Harper's Ferry VIRGINIA

Charleston 1740, 1822

Richmond 1801
Virginia 1831

NORTH CAROLINA

SOUTH CAROLINA

Stono 1739

GEORGIA

FLORIDA

1831- 1866 William Lloyd Garrison publishes the Liberator and organises American Anti-Slavery Society 1833. Nearly murdered by a Boston mob 1835. Declared U.S.Constitution which permitted slavery "a covenant with death and an agreement with hell"

Oberlin
OHIO 1803

1835 First college to admit negro students

MICHIGAN 1837

INDIANA 1816

ILLINOIS 1818
Alton

1859 Anti-slavery editor murdered

KENTUCKY

TENNESSEE

ALABAMA

MISS.

WISCONSIN 1848

MINNESOTA 1858

IOWA 1846

MISSOURI

ARKANSAS

LOUISIANA

1856 Abolitionist John Brown and sons murder five pro-slavery men

KANSAS TERRITORY
Pottawatomie

NEBRASKA TERRITORY

TEXAS

WASHINGTON TERRITORY 1848

OREGON TERRITORY 1848

UTAH TERRITORY

NEW MEXICO TERRITORY

CALIFORNIA 1850

300
Miles
0

● Negro uprisings
▨ States abolishing slavery
☐ Slave States

51

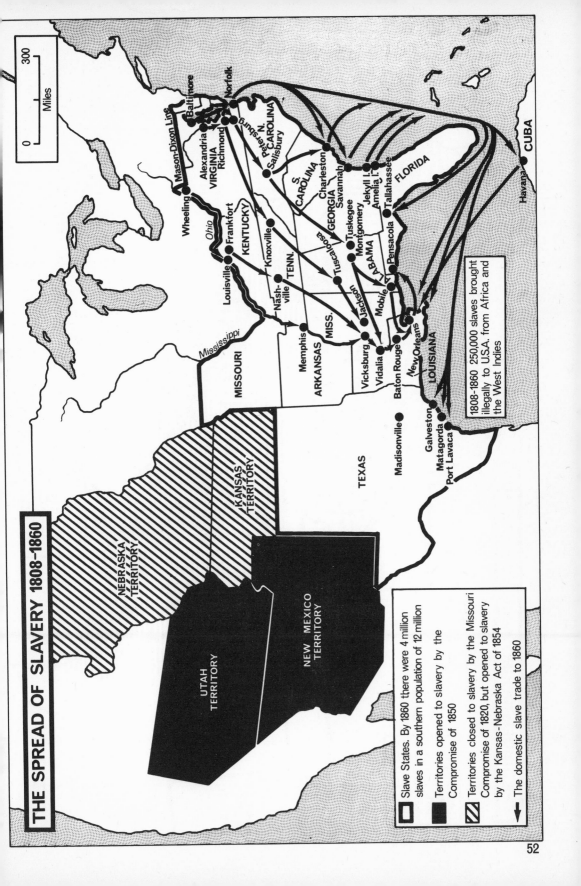

THE SPREAD OF SLAVERY 1808–1860

0   300 Miles

Mason-Dixon Line

Baltimore
Norfolk
Alexandria
VIRGINIA
Richmond
Wheeling
Ohio
Petersburg
N. CAROLINA
Salisbury
S. CAROLINA
Charleston
Savannah
GEORGIA
Jekyll I.
Amelia I.
Tallahassee
FLORIDA
CUBA
Havana
Frankfort
KENTUCKY
Louisville
Knoxville
TENN.
Nashville
Tuscaloosa
Tuskegee
Montgomery
ALABAMA
Pensacola
Mobile
Jackson
MISS.
Memphis
ARKANSAS
Vicksburg
Vidalia
Baton Rouge
New Orleans
LOUISIANA
MISSOURI

1808–1860 250,000 slaves brought
illegally to U.S.A. from Africa and
the West Indies

Madisonville
Galveston
Matagorda
Port Lavaca

TEXAS

KANSAS
TERRITORY

NEBRASKA
TERRITORY

UTAH
TERRITORY

NEW MEXICO
TERRITORY

☐   Slave States. By 1860 there were 4 million
slaves in a southern population of 12 million

■   Territories opened to slavery by the
Compromise of 1850

▨   Territories closed to slavery by the Missouri
Compromise of 1820, but opened to slavery
by the Kansas-Nebraska Act of 1854

→   The domestic slave trade to 1860

Mississippi

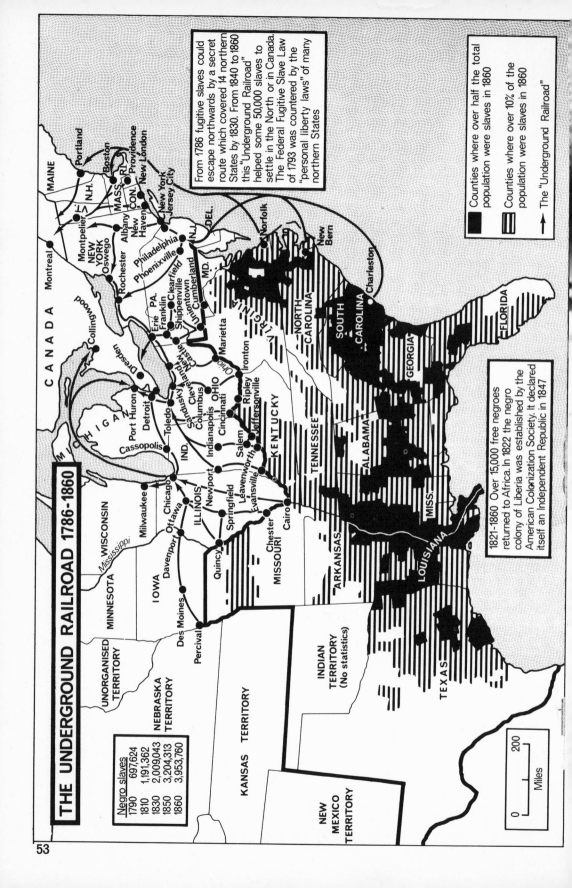

THE UNDERGROUND RAILROAD 1786-1860

From 1786 fugitive slaves could escape northwards by a secret route which covered 14 northern States by 1830. From 1840 to 1860 this "Underground Railroad" helped some 50,000 slaves to settle in the North or in Canada. The Federal Fugitive Slave Law of 1793 was countered by the "personal liberty laws" of many northern States

■ Counties where over half the total population were slaves in 1860

▥ Counties where over 10% of the population were slaves in 1860

→ The "Underground Railroad"

1821-1860 Over 15,000 free negroes returned to Africa. In 1822 the negro colony of Liberia was established by the American Colonization Society. It declared itself an Independent Republic in 1847

Negro slaves
1790   697,624
1810 1,191,362
1830 2,009,043
1850 3,204,313
1860 3,953,760

CANADA

MAINE
Portland
Montpelier N.H.
MASS. Boston
CON. Providence R.I.
New New London
Albany Haven
Oswego New York
Rochester Jersey City
NEW N.J.
YORK Philadelphia
Phoenixville
DEL.
PA. Clearfield
Erie Shippenville
Franklin Uniontown
Cumberland
MD.
Marietta
VIRGINIA
Norfolk
New Bern
NORTH
CAROLINA
SOUTH
CAROLINA
Charleston
GEORGIA
FLORIDA

Montreal
Collingwood
Dresden
Port Huron
Detroit
Toledo
Cassopolis
MICHIGAN
Sandusky
Cleveland
New Lisbon
OHIO Ironton
Columbus Ripley
Cincinnati Jeffersonville
IND. Salem
Indianapolis
KENTUCKY
TENNESSEE
ALABAMA
MISS.

Milwaukee
WISCONSIN
Chicago
Ottawa
ILLINOIS
Newport
Springfield
Leavenworth Evansville
Quincy Chester Cairo
Davenport
IOWA
MISSOURI
ARKANSAS
LOUISIANA
TEXAS

Des Moines
Percival
MINNESOTA
UNORGANISED
TERRITORY
NEBRASKA
TERRITORY
Mississippi

KANSAS TERRITORY

INDIAN
TERRITORY
(No statistics)

NEW
MEXICO
TERRITORY

0   200
Miles

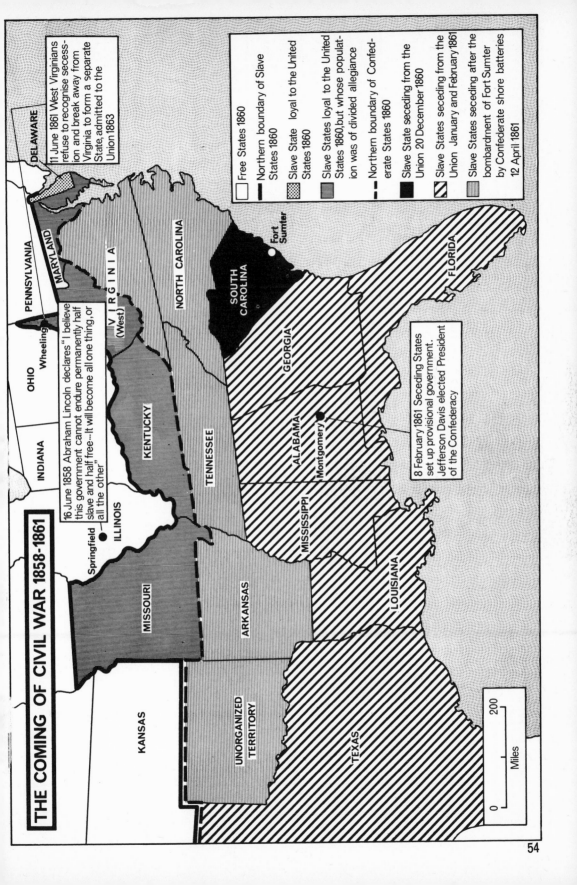

THE COMING OF CIVIL WAR 1858-1861

11 June 1861 West Virginians refuse to recognise secession and break away from Virginia to form a separate State, admitted to the Union 1863

□	Free States 1860
▮	Northern boundary of Slave States 1860
▦	Slave State loyal to the United States 1860
▥	Slave States loyal to the United States 1860, but whose population was of divided allegiance
┊	Northern boundary of Confederate States 1860
■	Slave State seceding from the Union 20 December 1860
▨	Slave States seceding from the Union January and February 1861
▒	Slave States seceding after the bombardment of Fort Sumter by Confederate shore batteries 12 April 1861

16 June 1858 Abraham Lincoln declares "I believe this government cannot endure permanently half slave and half free...It will become all one thing, or all the other"

8 February 1861 Seceding States set up provisional government. Jefferson Davis elected President of the Confederacy

DELAWARE

PENNSYLVANIA

MARYLAND

OHIO
Wheeling

VIRGINIA

VIRGINIA
(West)

NORTH CAROLINA

INDIANA

KENTUCKY

TENNESSEE

SOUTH CAROLINA

Fort Sumter

GEORGIA

FLORIDA

ILLINOIS
● Springfield

MISSOURI

ALABAMA

MISSISSIPPI

● Montgomery

ARKANSAS

LOUISIANA

KANSAS

UNORGANIZED TERRITORY

TEXAS

0   200
Miles

54

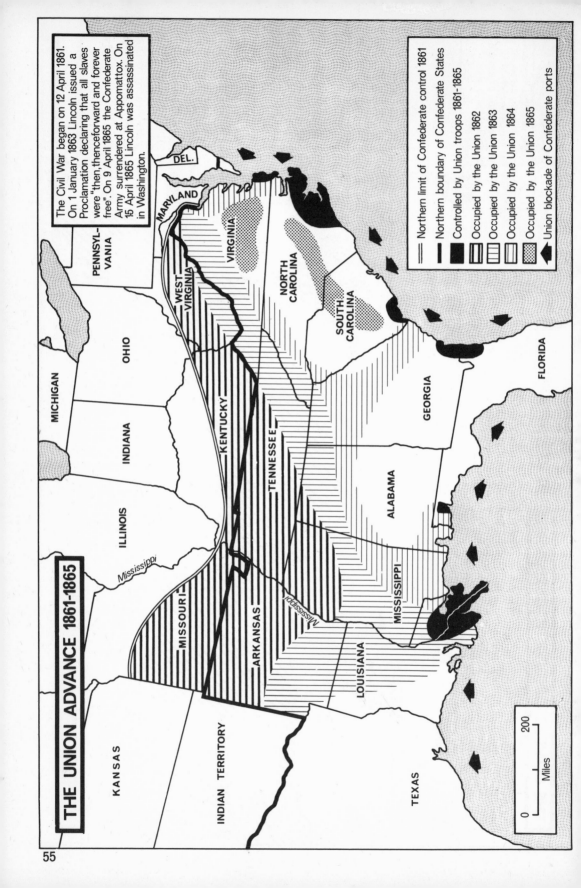

THE UNION ADVANCE 1861-1865

The Civil War began on 12 April 1861. On 1 January 1863 Lincoln issued a Proclamation declaring that all slaves were "then, thenceforward and forever free." On 9 April 1865 the Confederate Army surrendered at Appomattox. On 15 April 1865 Lincoln was assassinated in Washington.

Northern limit of Confederate control 1861
Northern boundary of Confederate States
Controlled by Union troops 1861-1865
Occupied by the Union 1862
Occupied by the Union 1863
Occupied by the Union 1864
Occupied by the Union 1865
Union blockade of Confederate ports

PENNSYL-VANIA

DEL.

MARYLAND

MICHIGAN

OHIO

WEST VIRGINIA

VIRGINIA

NORTH CAROLINA

SOUTH CAROLINA

INDIANA

KENTUCKY

TENNESSEE

GEORGIA

FLORIDA

ILLINOIS

Mississippi

ALABAMA

MISSOURI

ARKANSAS

Mississippi

MISSISSIPPI

LOUISIANA

KANSAS

INDIAN TERRITORY

TEXAS

0   200
Miles

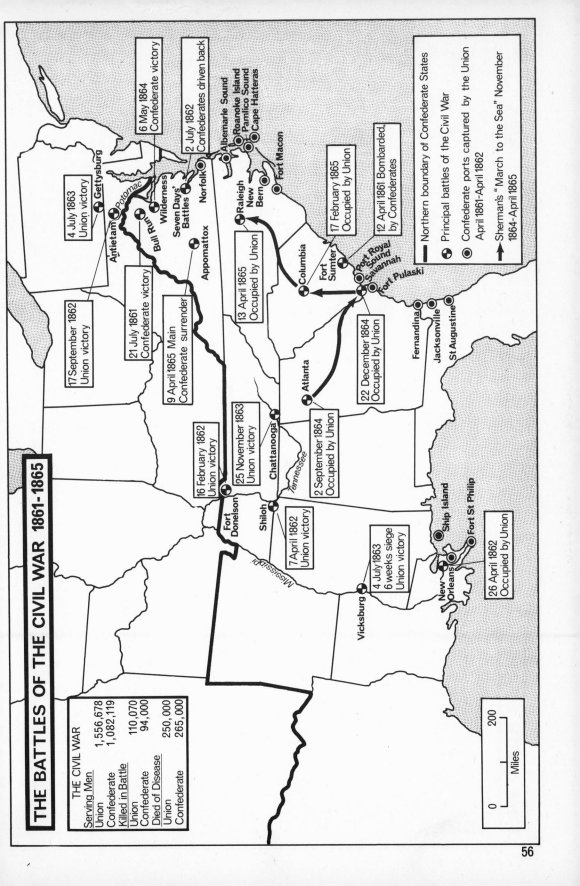

THE BATTLES OF THE CIVIL WAR 1861-1865

THE CIVIL WAR
Serving Men
Union 1,556,678
Confederate 1,082,119
Killed in Battle
Union 110,070
Confederate 94,000
Died of Disease
Union 250,000
Confederate 265,000

Miles
0   200

6 May 1864 Confederate victory

2 July 1862 Confederates driven back

Albemarle Sound
Roanoke Island
Pamlico Sound
Cape Hatteras

Fort Macon

17 February 1865 Occupied by Union

12 April 1861 Bombarded, by Confederates

— Northern boundary of Confederate States
⊕ Principal battles of the Civil War
◉ Confederate ports captured by the Union April 1861-April 1862
→ Shermans "March to the Sea" November 1864-April 1865

4 July 1863 Union victory

Gettysburg

Potomac

Antietam
Bull Run
Wilderness
Seven Days' Battles
Norfolk

Raleigh
New Bern

Fort Sumter
Port Royal Sound
Savannah
Fort Pulaski

17 September 1862 Union victory

21 July 1861 Confederate victory

Appomattox

9 April 1865 Main Confederate surrender

13 April 1865 Occupied by Union

Columbia

Fernandina
Jacksonville
St Augustine

22 December 1864 Occupied by Union

16 February 1862 Union victory

25 November 1863 Union victory

Chattanooga

Tennessee

Atlanta

2 September 1864 Occupied by Union

Fort Donelson
Shiloh

7 April 1862 Union victory

Mississippi

4 July 1863 6 weeks siege Union victory

Vicksburg

Ship Island
Fort St Philip

New Orleans

26 April 1862 Occupied by Union

56

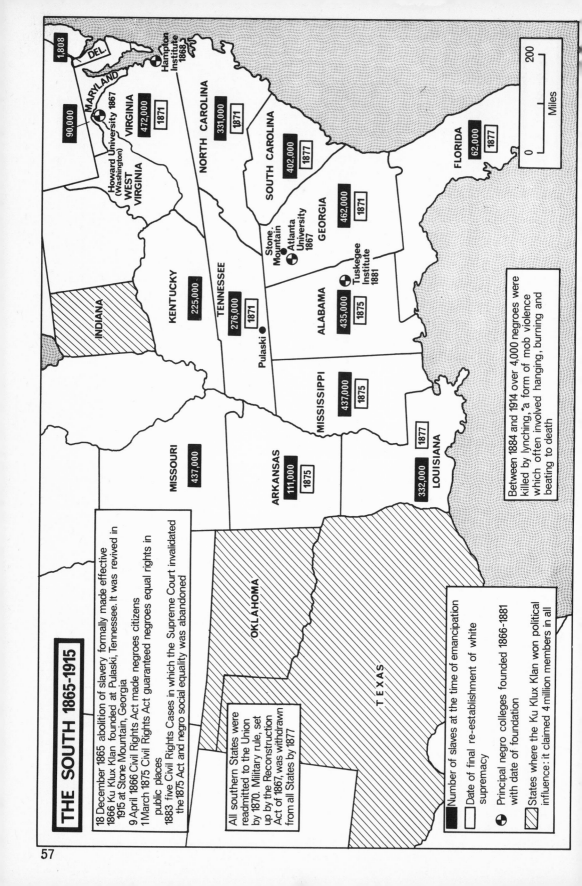

THE SOUTH 1865-1915

18 December 1865 abolition of slavery formally made effective
1866 Ku Klux Klan founded at Pulaski, Tennessee. It was revived in 1915 at Stone Mountain, Georgia
9 April 1866 Civil Rights Act made negroes citizens
1 March 1875 Civil Rights Act guaranteed negroes equal rights in public places
1883 five Civil Rights Cases in which the Supreme Court invalidated the 1875 Act and negro social equality was abandoned

All southern States were readmitted to the Union by 1870. Military rule, set up by the Reconstruction Act of 1867, was withdrawn from all States by 1877

Between 1884 and 1914 over 4,000 negroes were killed by lynching, "a form of mob violence which often involved hanging, burning and beating to death

■ Number of slaves at the time of emancipation

□ Date of final re-establishment of white supremacy

✪ Principal negro colleges founded 1866-1881 with date of foundation

▨ States where the Ku Klux Klan won political influence : it claimed 4 million members in all

States and data

DEL 1,808

MARYLAND 90,000

Howard University 1867 (Washington)

Hampton Institute 1868

VIRGINIA 472,000 | 1871

WEST VIRGINIA

NORTH CAROLINA 331,000 | 1871

SOUTH CAROLINA 402,000 | 1877

FLORIDA 62,000 | 1877

GEORGIA 462,000 | 1871

Stone Mountain

Atlanta University 1867

Tuskegee Institute 1881

ALABAMA 435,000 | 1875

KENTUCKY

TENNESSEE 276,000 | 1871

Pulaski ●

MISSISSIPPI 437,000 | 1875

INDIANA

MISSOURI 437,000

ARKANSAS 111,000 | 1875

LOUISIANA 332,000 | 1877

OKLAHOMA

TEXAS

200 | 0 Miles

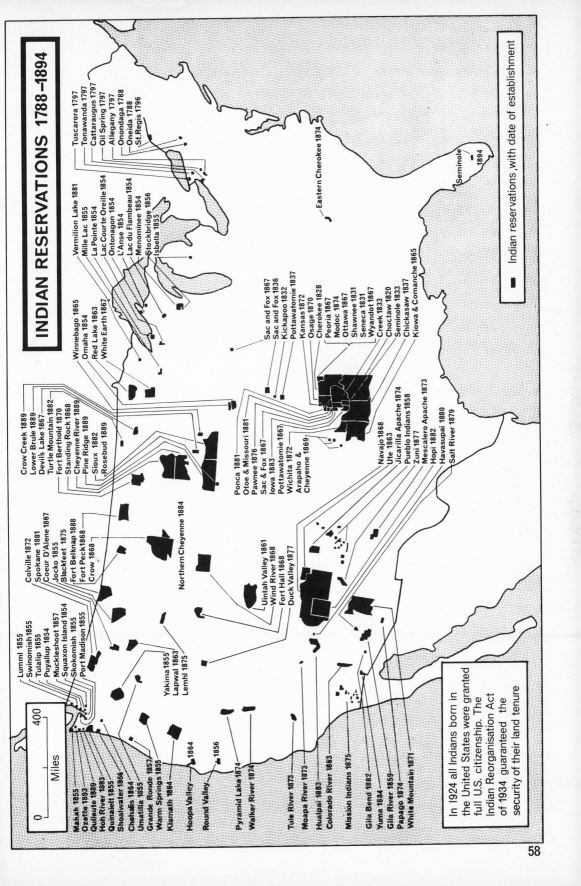

INDIAN RESERVATIONS 1788–1894

0 — 400 Miles

Tuscarora 1797
Tonawanda 1797
Cattaraugus 1797
Oil Spring 1797
Allegany 1797
Onondaga 1788
Oneida 1788
St.Regis 1796

Vermillion Lake 1881
Mille Lac 1855
La Pointe 1854
Lac Courte Oreille 1854
Ontonagon 1854
L'Anse 1854
Lac du Flambeau 1854
Menominee 1854
Stockbridge 1856
Isbella 1855

Winnebago 1865
Omaha 1854
Red Lake 1863
White Earth 1867

Eastern Cherokee 1874

Seminole 1894

Sac and Fox 1867
Sac and Fox 1836
Kickapoo 1832
Pottawatomie 1837
Kansas 1872
Osage 1870
Cherokee 1828
Peoria 1867
Modoc 1874
Ottawa 1867
Shawnee 1831
Seneca 1831
Wyandot 1867
Creek 1833
Choctaw 1820
Seminole 1833
Chickasaw 1837
Kiowa & Comanche 1865

Crow Creek 1889
Lower Brule 1889
Devil's Lake 1867
Turtle Mountain 1882
Standing Rock 1870
Fort Berthold 1870
Cheyenne River 1889
Pine Ridge 1889
Sioux 1889
Rosebud 1889

Colville 1872
Spokane 1881
Coeur D'Alene 1867
Jocko 1855
Blackfeet 1875
Fort Belknap 1888
Fort Peck 1868
Crow 1868

Northern Cheyenne 1884

Ponca 1881
Otoe & Missouri 1881
Pawnee 1876
Sac & Fox 1867
Iowa 1883
Pottawatomie 1867
Wichita 1872
Arapaho &
Cheyenne 1869

Navajo 1868
Ute 1863
Jicarilla Apache 1874
Pueblo Indians 1858
Zuni 1877
Mescalero Apache 1873
Hopi 1882
Havasupai 1880
Salt River 1879

Lumml 1855
Swinomish 1855
Tulalip 1855
Puyallup 1854
Muckleshoot 1857
Squaxon Island 1854
Skokomish 1855
Port Madison 1855

Yakima 1855
Lapwal 1863
Lemhi 1875

Uintah Valley 1861
Wind River 1868
Fort Hall 1868
Duck Valley 1877

Makah 1855
Ozetta 1893
Quileute 1889
Hoh River 1893
Quinalalt 1855
Shoalwater 1866
Chehalis 1864
Umatilla 1855
Grande Ronde 1857
Warm Springs 1855
Klamath 1864

Hoopa Valley 1864
Round Valley 1856

Pyramid Lake 1874
Walker River 1874

1864
1856

Tule River 1873
Moapa River 1873
Hualapai 1883
Colorado River 1865
Mission Indians 1875

Gila Bend 1882
Yuma 1884
Gila River 1859
Papago 1874
White Mountain 1871

■ — Indian reservations, with date of establishment

In 1924 all Indians born in
the United States were granted
full U.S. citizenship. The
Indian Reorganisation Act
of 1934 guaranteed the
security of their land tenure

58

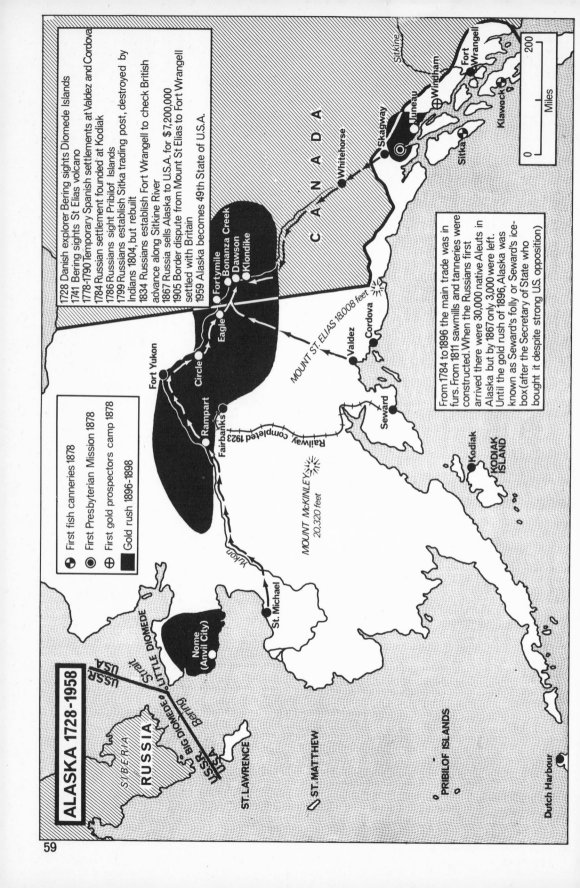

ALASKA 1728-1958

1728 Danish explorer Bering sights Diomede Islands
1741 Bering sights St Elias volcano
1778-1790 Temporary Spanish settlements at Valdez and Cordova
1784 Russian settlement founded at Kodiak
1786 Russians sight Pribilof Islands
1799 Russians establish Sitka trading post, destroyed by Indians 1804, but rebuilt
1834 Russians establish Fort Wrangell to check British advance along Sitkine River
1867 Russia sells Alaska to U.S.A. for $7,200,000
1905 Border dispute from Mount St Elias to Fort Wrangell settled with Britain
1959 Alaska becomes 49th State of U.S.A.

From 1784 to 1896 the main trade was in furs. From 1811 sawmills and tanneries were constructed. When the Russians first arrived there were 30,000 native Aleuts in Alaska but by 1867 only 3,000 were left. Until the gold rush of 1896, Alaska was known as Seward's folly or Seward's icebox (after the Secretary of State who bought it despite strong U.S. opposition)

○ First fish canneries 1878
◎ First Presbyterian Mission 1878
⊕ First gold prospectors camp 1878
■ Gold rush 1896-1898

CANADA

RUSSIA

SIBERIA

USSR / USA

Bering Strait

BIG DIOMEDE

LITTLE DIOMEDE

Nome (Anvil City)

St. Michael

ST. LAWRENCE

ST. MATTHEW

PRIBILOF ISLANDS

Dutch Harbour

KODIAK ISLAND

Kodiak

Seward

Valdez

Cordova

MOUNT ST. ELIAS 18,008 feet

MOUNT McKINLEY 20,320 feet

Fairbanks

Rampart

Circle

Fort Yukon

Eagle

Fortymile

Bonanza Creek

Dawson

Klondike

Yukon

Railway completed 1923

Whitehorse

Skagway

Juneau

Windham

Fort Wrangell

Sitka

Klawock

Sitkine

Miles

0   200

59

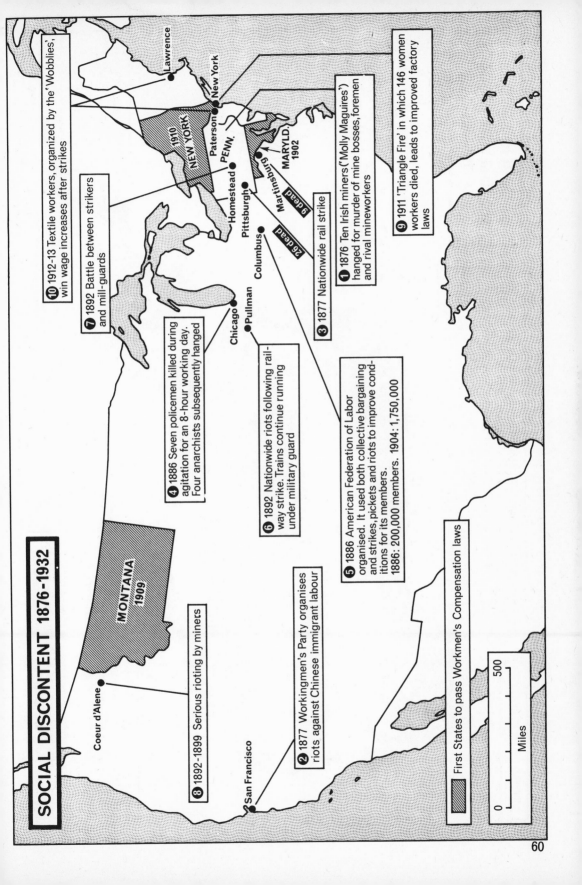

SOCIAL DISCONTENT 1876-1932

10 1912-13 Textile workers, organized by the 'Wobblies', win wage increases after strikes

7 1892 Battle between strikers and mill-guards

4 1886 Seven policemen killed during agitation for an 8-hour working day. Four anarchists subsequently hanged

6 1892 Nationwide riots following railway strike. Trains continue running under military guard

5 1886 American Federation of Labor organised. It used both collective bargaining and strikes, pickets and riots to improve conditions for its members. 1886: 200,000 members. 1904: 1,750,000

8 1892-1899 Serious rioting by miners

2 1877 Workingmen's Party organises riots against Chinese immigrant labour

1 1876 Ten Irish miners ('Molly Maguires') hanged for murder of mine bosses, foremen and rival mineworkers

9 1911 'Triangle Fire' in which 146 women workers died, leads to improved factory laws

3 1877 Nationwide rail strike

Lawrence

New York

Paterson

PENN.

NEW YORK
1910

MARYLD.
1902

9 dead

26 dead

Homestead

Pittsburgh

Martinsburg

Columbus

Pullman

Chicago

MONTANA
1909

Coeur d'Alene

San Francisco

First States to pass Workmen's Compensation laws

Miles

0   500

60

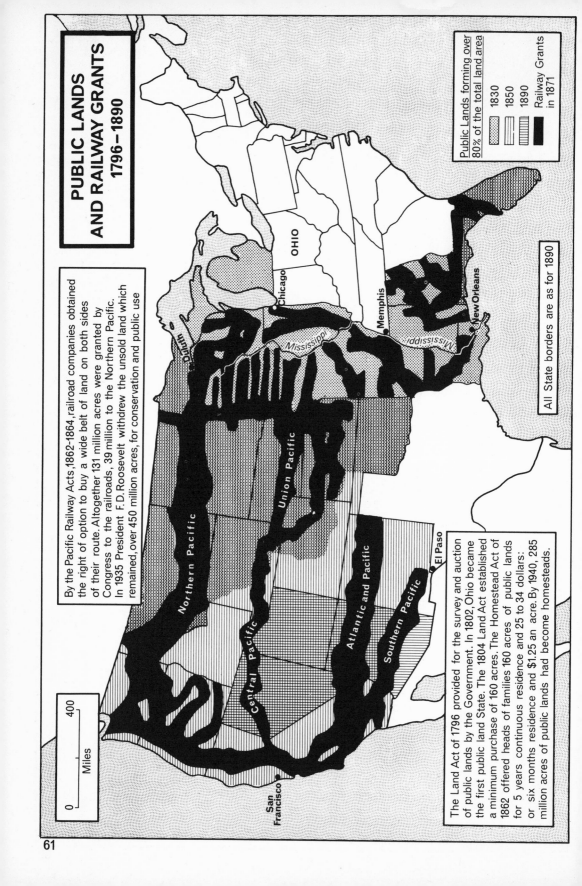

PUBLIC LANDS AND RAILWAY GRANTS 1796–1890

By the Pacific Railway Acts, 1862-1864, railroad companies obtained the right of option to buy a wide belt of land on both sides of their route. Altogether 131 million acres were granted by Congress to the railroads, 39 million to the Northern Pacific. In 1935 President F.D. Roosevelt withdrew the unsold land which remained, over 450 million acres, for conservation and public use

The Land Act of 1796 provided for the survey and auction of public lands by the Government. In 1802, Ohio became the first public land State. The 1804 Land Act established a minimum purchase of 160 acres. The Homestead Act of 1862 offered heads of families 160 acres of public lands for 5 years continuous residence and 25 to 34 dollars: or six months residence and $1.25 an acre. By 1940, 285 million acres of public lands had become homesteads.

All State borders are as for 1890

Public Lands forming over 80% of the total land area
1830
1850
1890
Railway Grants in 1871

OHIO

Duluth
Chicago
Memphis
New Orleans
Mississippi
Mississippi

Northern Pacific
Union Pacific
Central Pacific
Atlantic and Pacific
Southern Pacific
El Paso
San Francisco

Miles
0   400

61

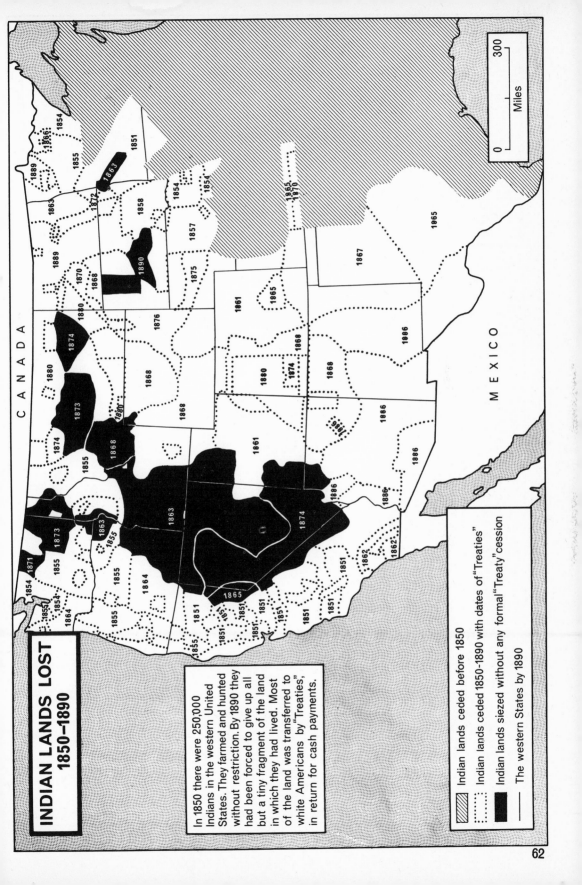

INDIAN LANDS LOST 1850–1890

In 1850 there were 250,000 Indians in the western United States. They farmed and hunted without restriction. By 1890 they had been forced to give up all but a tiny fragment of the land in which they had lived. Most of the land was transferred to white Americans by "Treaties", in return for cash payments.

300

Miles

0

CANADA

MEXICO

Indian lands ceded before 1850

Indian lands ceded 1850-1890 with dates of "Treaties"

Indian lands siezed without any formal "Treaty" cession

The western States by 1890

62

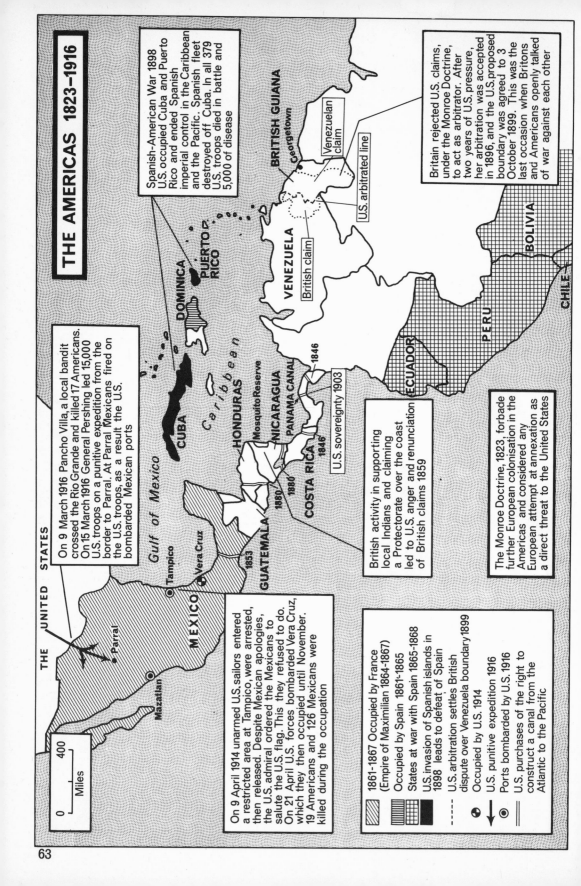

THE AMERICAS 1823–1916

Spanish-American War 1898 U.S. occupied Cuba and Puerto Rico and ended Spanish imperial control in the Caribbean and the Pacific. Spanish fleet destroyed off Cuba. In all 379 U.S. troops died in battle and 5,000 of disease

Britain rejected U.S. claims, under the Monroe Doctrine, to act as arbitrator. After two years of U.S. pressure, her arbitration was accepted in 1896, and the U.S. proposed boundary was agreed to 3 October 1899. This was the last occasion when Britons and Americans openly talked of war against each other

On 9 March 1916 Pancho Villa, a local bandit crossed the Rio Grande and killed 17 Americans. On 15 March 1916 General Pershing led 15,000 U.S. troops on a punitive expedition from the border to Parral. At Parral Mexicans fired on the U.S. troops, as a result the U.S. bombarded Mexican ports

BRITISH GUIANA

Georgetown

Venezuelan claim

U.S. arbitrated line

VENEZUELA

British claim

DOMINICA

PUERTO RICO

CUBA

Gulf of Mexico

Caribbean Sea

MEXICO

Parral

Mazatlan

Tampico

Vera Cruz

1853

GUATEMALA

HONDURAS

Mosquito Reserve

1846

NICARAGUA

PANAMA CANAL

1880

1880

1846

COSTA RICA

U.S. sovereignty 1903

ECUADOR

PERU

BOLIVIA

CHILE

THE UNITED STATES

British activity in supporting local Indians and claiming a Protectorate over the coast led to U.S. anger and renunciation of British claims 1859

The Monroe Doctrine, 1823, forbade further European colonisation in the Americas and considered any European attempt at annexation as a direct threat to the United States

On 9 April 1914 unarmed U.S. sailors entered a restricted area at Tampico, were arrested, then released. Despite Mexican apologies, the U.S. admiral ordered the Mexicans to salute the U.S. flag. This they refused to do. On 21 April U.S. forces bombarded Vera Cruz, which they then occupied until November. 19 Americans and 126 Mexicans were killed during the occupation

0   400
Miles

1861–1867 Occupied by France (Empire of Maximilian 1864–1867)

Occupied by Spain 1861–1865

States at war with Spain 1865–1868

U.S. invasion of Spanish islands in 1898 leads to defeat of Spain

U.S. arbitration settles British dispute over Venezuela boundary 1899

Occupied by U.S. 1914

U.S. punitive expedition 1916

Ports bombarded by U.S. 1916

U.S. purchases of the right to construct a canal from the Atlantic to the Pacific

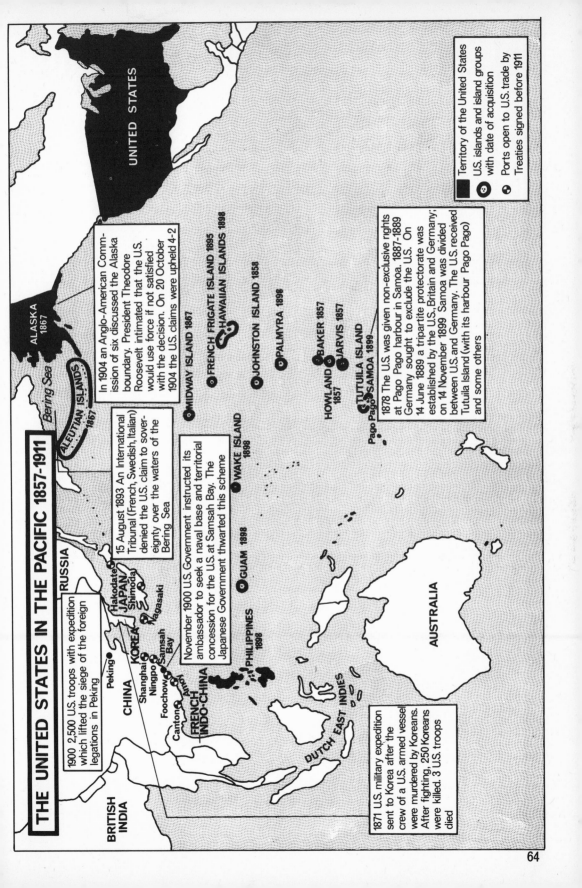

THE UNITED STATES IN THE PACIFIC 1857-1911

Territory of the United States

U.S. islands and island groups with date of acquisition

Ports open to U.S. trade by Treaties signed before 1911

UNITED STATES

RUSSIA

BRITISH INDIA

CHINA

JAPAN
Hakodate
Shimoda
Nagasaki

KOREA

Samsah Bay
Shanghai
Ningpo
Foochow
Amoy
Canton

Peking

FRENCH INDO-CHINA

PHILIPPINES 1898

DUTCH EAST INDIES

AUSTRALIA

ALASKA 1867

Bering Sea

ALEUTIAN ISLANDS 1857

MIDWAY ISLAND 1867

FRENCH FRIGATE ISLAND 1895

HAWAIIAN ISLANDS 1898

JOHNSTON ISLAND 1858

PALMYRA 1898

BAKER 1857

HOWLAND 1857

JARVIS 1857

TUTUILA ISLAND
Pago Pago SAMOA 1899

WAKE ISLAND 1898

GUAM 1898

1900 2,500 U.S. troops with expedition which lifted the siege of the foreign legations in Peking

15 August 1893 An International Tribunal (French, Swedish, Italian) denied the U.S. claim to sovereignty over the waters of the Bering Sea

November 1900 U.S. Government instructed its ambassador to seek a naval base and territorial concession for the U.S. at Samsah Bay. The Japanese Government thwarted this scheme

In 1904 an Anglo-American Commission of six discussed the Alaska boundary. President Theodore Roosevelt intimated that the U.S. would use force if not satisfied with the decision. On 20 October 1904 the U.S. claims were upheld 4-2

1878 The U.S. was given non-exclusive rights at Pago Pago harbour in Samoa. 1887-1889 Germany sought to exclude the U.S. On 14 June 1889 a tripartite protectorate was established by the U.S., Britain and Germany; on 14 November 1899 Samoa was divided between U.S. and Germany. The U.S. received Tutuila Island (with its harbour Pago Pago) and some others

1871 U.S. military expedition sent to Korea after the crew of a U.S. armed vessel were murdered by Koreans. After fighting, 250 Koreans were killed. 3 U.S. troops died

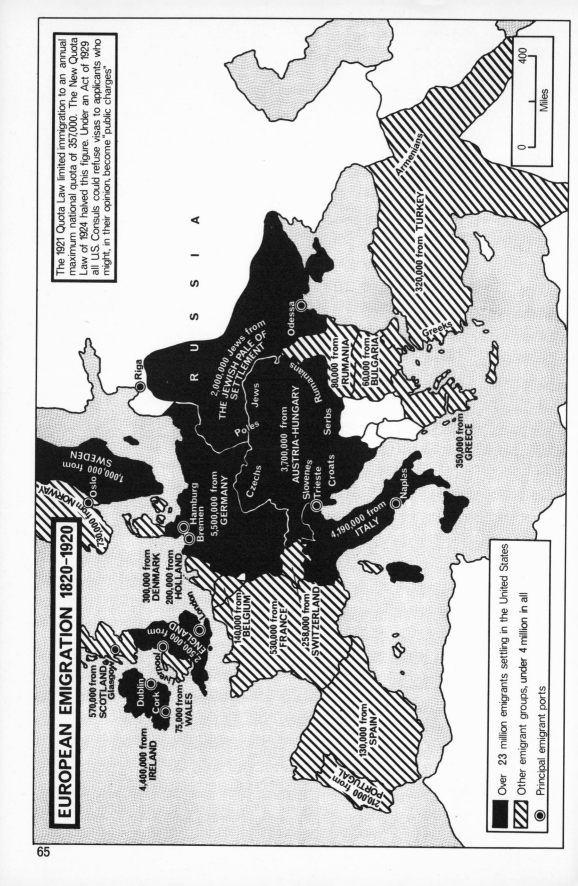

EUROPEAN EMIGRATION 1820–1920

The 1921 Quota Law limited immigration to an annual maximum national quota of 357,000. The New Quota Law of 1924 halved this figure. Under an Act of 1929 all U.S. Consuls could refuse visas to applicants who might, in their opinion, become "public charges"

400

Miles

R U S S I A

2,000,000 Jews from THE JEWISH PALE OF SETTLEMENT

Odessa

Riga

320,000 from TURKEY

Armenians

Greeks

80,000 from RUMANIA

60,000 from BULGARIA

350,000 from GREECE

Rumanians

Poles

Jews

Czechs

Serbs

Slovenes

Croats

Trieste

3,700,000 from AUSTRIA-HUNGARY

Naples

4,190,000 from ITALY

5,500,000 from GERMANY

Hamburg

Bremen

1,000,000 from SWEDEN

Oslo

120,000 from NORWAY

300,000 from DENMARK

200,000 from HOLLAND

140,000 from BELGIUM

530,000 from FRANCE

258,000 from SWITZERLAND

130,000 from SPAIN

210,000 from PORTUGAL

570,000 from SCOTLAND

Glasgow

London

2,500,000 from ENGLAND

Liverpool

Dublin

Cork

4,400,000 from IRELAND

75,000 from WALES

■ Over 23 million emigrants settling in the United States

▨ Other emigrant groups, under 4 million in all

◉ Principal emigrant ports

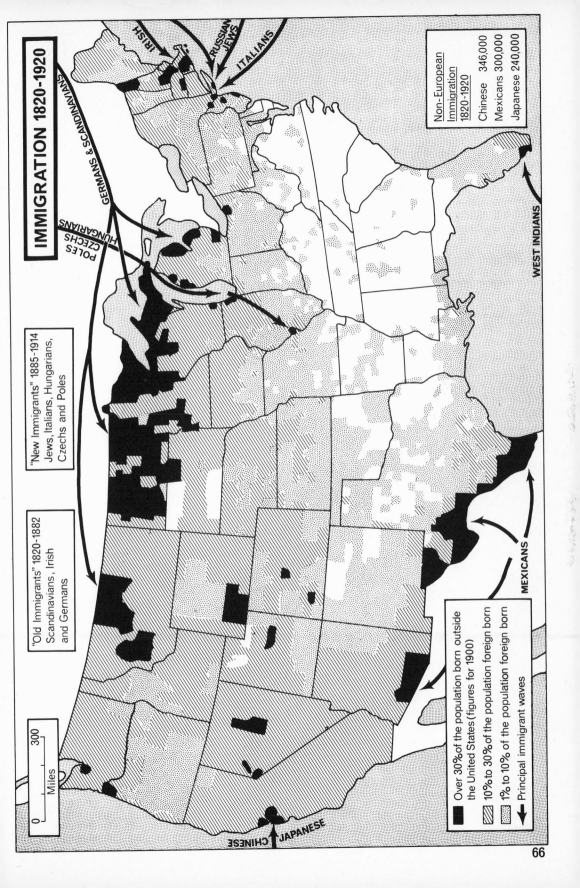

IMMIGRATION 1820-1920

IRISH

RUSSIAN JEWS

ITALIANS

GERMANS & SCANDINAVIANS

POLES
CZECHS
HUNGARIANS

Non-European
Immigration
1820-1920

Chinese   346,000
Mexicans   300,000
Japanese   240,000

"New Immigrants" 1885-1914
Jews, Italians, Hungarians,
Czechs and Poles

"Old Immigrants" 1820-1882
Scandinavians, Irish
and Germans

WEST INDIANS

MEXICANS

300

0   Miles

Over 30% of the population born outside
the United States (figures for 1900)

10% to 30% of the population foreign born

1% to 10% of the population foreign born

Principal immigrant waves

CHINESE   JAPANESE

66

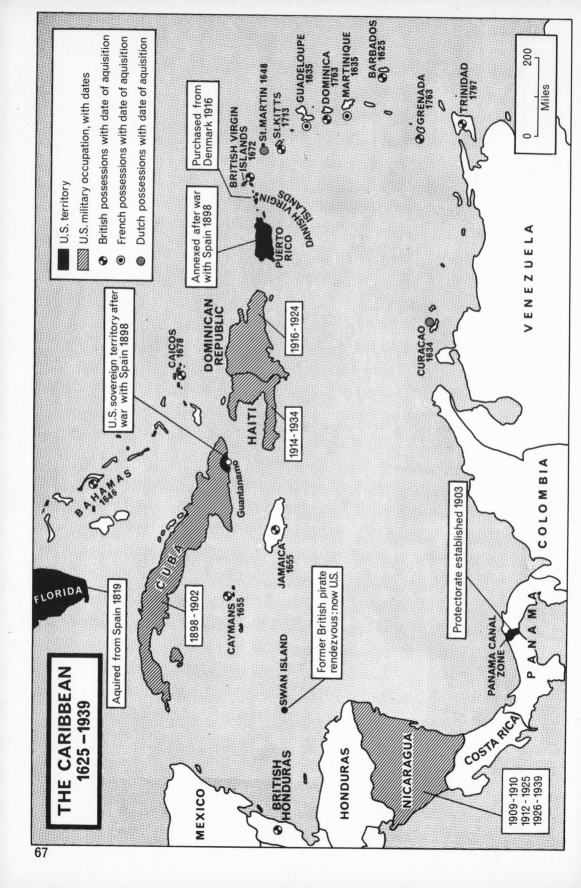

THE CARIBBEAN 1625–1939

U.S. territory

U.S. military occupation, with dates

British possessions with date of aquisition

French possessions with date of aquisition

Dutch possessions with date of aquisition

Purchased from Denmark 1916

Annexed after war with Spain 1898

Aquired from Spain 1819

U.S. sovereign territory after war with Spain 1898

1916–1924

1914–1934

1898–1902

Former British pirate rendezvous: now U.S.

Protectorate established 1903

1909–1910
1912–1925
1926–1939

200

Miles

0

FLORIDA

MEXICO

BRITISH HONDURAS

HONDURAS

NICARAGUA

COSTA RICA

PANAMA

PANAMA CANAL ZONE

COLOMBIA

VENEZUELA

BAHAMAS 1646

CUBA

Guantanamo

CAYMANS 1655

SWAN ISLAND

JAMAICA 1655

CAICOS 1678

HAITI

DOMINICAN REPUBLIC

PUERTO RICO

DANISH VIRGIN ISLANDS

BRITISH VIRGIN ISLANDS 1672

St.MARTIN 1648

St.KITTS 1713

GUADELOUPE 1635

DOMINICA 1763

MARTINIQUE 1635

BARBADOS 1625

GRENADA 1763

TRINIDAD 1797

CURACAO 1634

67

THE PANAMA CANAL ZONE PROTECTORATE 1903

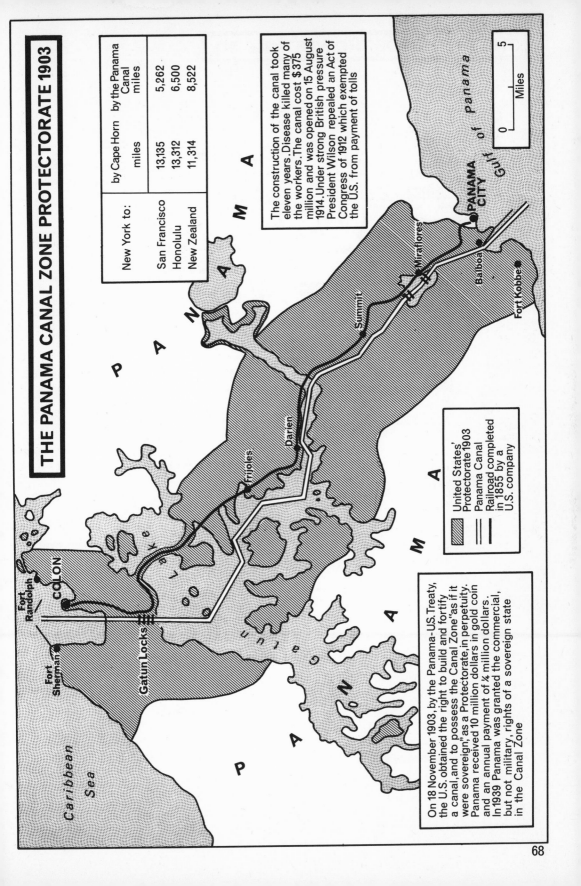

New York to:	by Cape Horn miles	by the Panama Canal miles
San Francisco	13,135	5,262
Honolulu	13,312	6,500
New Zealand	11,314	8,522

The construction of the canal took eleven years. Disease killed many of the workers. The canal cost $375 million and was opened on 15 August 1914. Under strong British pressure President Wilson repealed an Act of Congress of 1912 which exempted the U.S. from payment of tolls

P A N A M A

PANAMA CITY

Gulf of Panama

Miraflores

Summit

Balboa

Fort Kobbe

Darien

Trijoles

P A N A M A

Gatun Locks

COLON

Fort Randolph

Fort Sherman

Caribbean Sea

P A N A M A

United States' Protectorate 1903

Panama Canal

Railroad completed in 1855 by a U.S. company

0   5
Miles

On 18 November 1903, by the Panama-U.S. Treaty, the U.S. obtained the right to build and fortify a canal, and to possess the Canal Zone "as if it were sovereign", as a Protectorate, in perpetuity. Panama received 10 million dollars in gold coin and an annual payment of ¾ million dollars. In 1939 Panama was granted the commercial, but not military, rights of a sovereign state in the Canal Zone

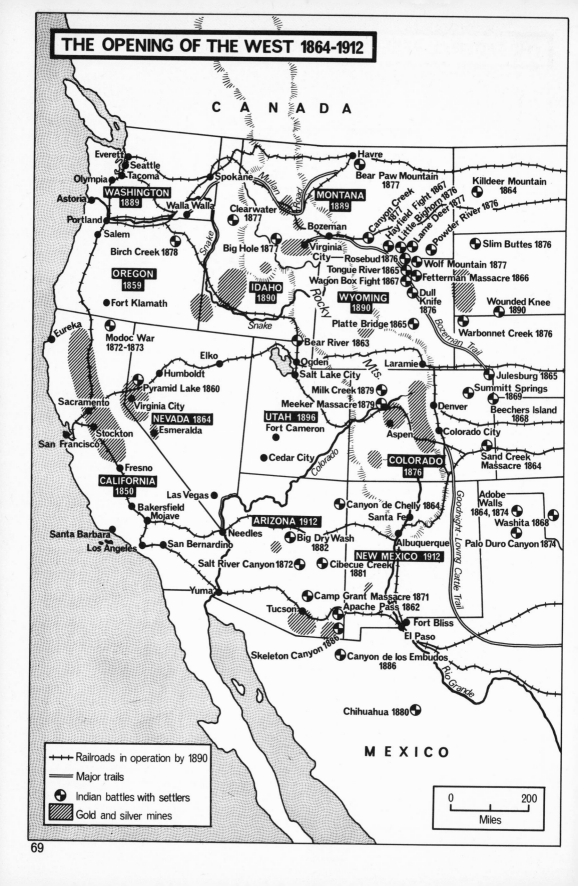

THE OPENING OF THE WEST 1864-1912

C A N A D A

Everett
Seattle
Olympia Tacoma
Astoria
WASHINGTON 1889
Portland
Walla Walla
Salem
Birch Creek 1878
OREGON 1859
Fort Klamath

Spokane
Mullan Road
Clearwater 1877
Bozeman
Big Hole 1877
Virginia City
IDAHO 1890

Havre
Bear Paw Mountain 1877
MONTANA 1889
Canyon Creek 1877
Hayfield Fight 1867
Little Bighorn 1876
Lame Deer 1877
Powder River 1876
Rosebud 1876
Tongue River 1865
Wagon Box Fight 1867
WYOMING 1890
Platte Bridge 1865
Dull Knife 1876

Killdeer Mountain 1864

Slim Buttes 1876
Wolf Mountain 1877
Fetterman Massacre 1866
Wounded Knee 1890
Warbonnet Creek 1876

Eureka
Modoc War 1872-1873
Elko
Humboldt
Pyramid Lake 1860
Sacramento
Virginia City
Stockton
San Francisco
NEVADA 1864
Esmeralda
Fresno
CALIFORNIA 1850
Las Vegas
Bakersfield
Mojave
Santa Barbara
Los Angeles
San Bernardino
Needles

Bear River 1863
Ogden
Salt Lake City
Milk Creek 1879
Meeker Massacre 1879
UTAH 1896
Fort Cameron
Aspen
Cedar City
COLORADO 1876

Laramie
Julesburg 1865
Summitt Springs 1869
Beechers Island 1868
Denver
Colorado City
Sand Creek Massacre 1864

Bozeman Trail

Canyon de Chelly 1864
Santa Fe
ARIZONA 1912
Big Dry Wash 1882
Salt River Canyon 1872
Cibecue Creek 1881
Albuquerque
NEW MEXICO 1912

Goodnight-Loving Cattle Trail

Adobe Walls 1864, 1874
Washita 1868
Palo Duro Canyon 1874

Yuma
Camp Grant Massacre 1871
Apache Pass 1862
Tucson
Fort Bliss
Skeleton Canyon 1886
Canyon de los Embudos 1886
El Paso

Rio Grande

Chihuahua 1880

M E X I C O

Rocky Mts.
Snake
Colorado

Railroads in operation by 1890
Major trails
Indian battles with settlers
Gold and silver mines

0   200
Miles

69

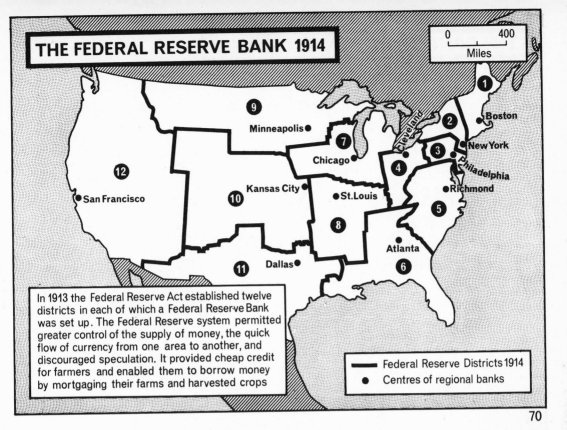

THE FEDERAL RESERVE BANK 1914

0 — 400
Miles

① Boston
② New York
③ Philadelphia
④ Cleveland
⑤ Richmond
⑥ Atlanta
⑦ Chicago
⑧ St.Louis
⑨ Minneapolis
⑩ Kansas City
⑪ Dallas
⑫ San Francisco

In 1913 the Federal Reserve Act established twelve districts in each of which a Federal Reserve Bank was set up. The Federal Reserve system permitted greater control of the supply of money, the quick flow of currency from one area to another, and discouraged speculation. It provided cheap credit for farmers and enabled them to borrow money by mortgaging their farms and harvested crops

—— Federal Reserve Districts 1914
● Centres of regional banks

70

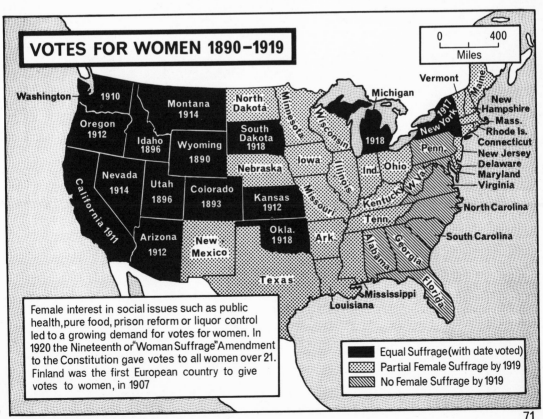

VOTES FOR WOMEN 1890–1919

0 — 400
Miles

Washington 1910
Oregon 1912
Montana 1914
North Dakota
South Dakota 1918
Michigan
Vermont
Maine
New York 1917
New Hampshire
Mass.
Rhode Is.
Connecticut
New Jersey
Delaware
Maryland
Virginia
Idaho 1896
Wyoming 1890
Minnesota
Wisconsin
1918
Penn.
Nevada 1914
Utah 1896
Colorado 1893
Nebraska
Iowa
Illinois
Ind.
Ohio
W.Va.
North Carolina
California 1911
Arizona 1912
New Mexico
Kansas 1912
Okla. 1918
Ark
Kentucky
Tenn.
South Carolina
Georgia
Florida
Texas
Alabama
Mississippi
Louisiana

Female interest in social issues such as public health, pure food, prison reform or liquor control led to a growing demand for votes for women. In 1920 the Nineteenth or "Woman Suffrage" Amendment to the Constitution gave votes to all women over 21. Finland was the first European country to give votes to women, in 1907

■ Equal Suffrage (with date voted)
▦ Partial Female Suffrage by 1919
▨ No Female Suffrage by 1919

71

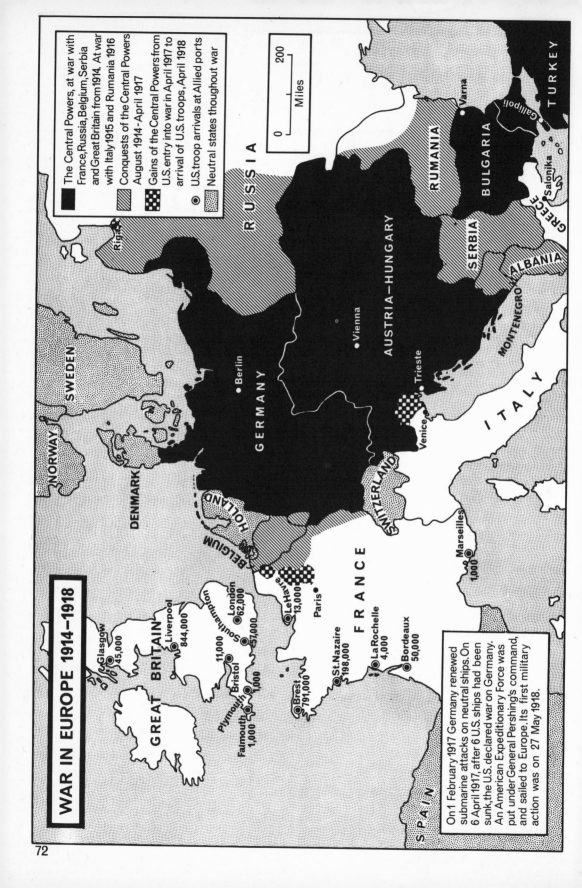

WAR IN EUROPE 1914-1918

The Central Powers, at war with France, Russia, Belgium, Serbia and Great Britain from 1914. At war with Italy 1915 and Rumania 1916

Conquests of the Central Powers August 1914 - April 1917

Gains of the Central Powers from U.S. entry into war in April 1917 to arrival of U.S. troops, April 1918

⊙ U.S. troop arrivals at Allied ports

Neutral states thoughout war

0   200
Miles

On 1 February 1917 Germany renewed submarine attacks on neutral ships. On 6 April 1917, after 6 U.S. ships had been sunk, the U.S. declared war on Germany. An American Expeditionary Force was put under General Pershing's command, and sailed to Europe. Its first military action was on 27 May 1918.

NORWAY

SWEDEN

DENMARK

RUSSIA

Riga

Berlin

GERMANY

HOLLAND

BELGIUM

GREAT BRITAIN

Glasgow
45,000
Liverpool
844,000
London
62,000
Southampton
37,000
Bristol
11,000
Plymouth
1,000
Falmouth
1,000
Le Havre
13,000
Paris
Brest
791,000
St. Nazaire
198,000
La Rochelle
4,000
Bordeaux
50,000

FRANCE

SWITZERLAND

AUSTRIA-HUNGARY

Vienna

Trieste

Venice

ITALY

Marseilles
1,000

SPAIN

RUMANIA

BULGARIA

Varna

Gallipoli

TURKEY

GREECE

Salonika

SERBIA

ALBANIA

MONTENEGRO

72

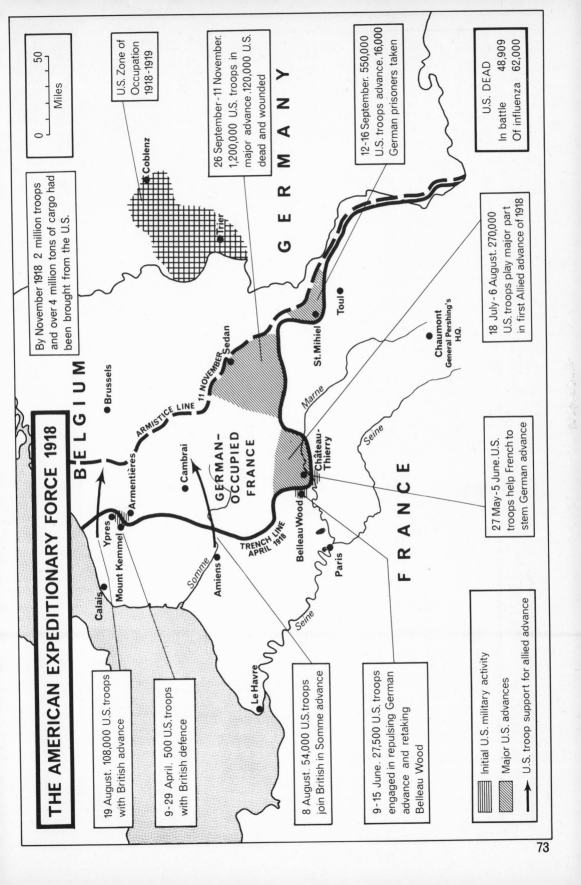

THE AMERICAN EXPEDITIONARY FORCE 1918

Scale: 0 — 50 Miles

U.S. Zone of Occupation 1918-1919

By November 1918 2 million troops and over 4 million tons of cargo had been brought from the U.S.

26 September - 11 November. 1,200,000 U.S. troops in major advance 120,000 U.S. dead and wounded

12-16 September. 550,000 U.S. troops advance. 16,000 German prisoners taken

U.S. DEAD
In battle   48,909
Of influenza 62,000

18 July - 6 August. 270,000 U.S. troops play major part in first Allied advance of 1918

27 May-5 June. U.S. troops help French to stem German advance

19 August. 108,000 U.S. troops with British advance

9 - 29 April. 500 U.S. troops with British defence

8 August. 54,000 U.S.troops join British in Somme advance

9-15 June. 27,500 U.S. troops engaged in repulsing German advance and retaking Belleau Wood

Initial U.S. military activity

Major U.S. advances

U.S. troop support for allied advance

GERMANY

BELGIUM

FRANCE

GERMAN-OCCUPIED FRANCE

ARMISTICE LINE

11 NOVEMBER

TRENCH LINE APRIL 1918

Coblenz

Trier

Brussels

Sedan

St.Mihiel

Toul

Chaumont
General Pershing's H.Q.

Cambrai

Armentières

Ypres

Mount Kemmel

Calais

Amiens

Le Havre

Paris

Belleau Wood

Château-Thierry

Marne

Seine

Seine

Somme

73

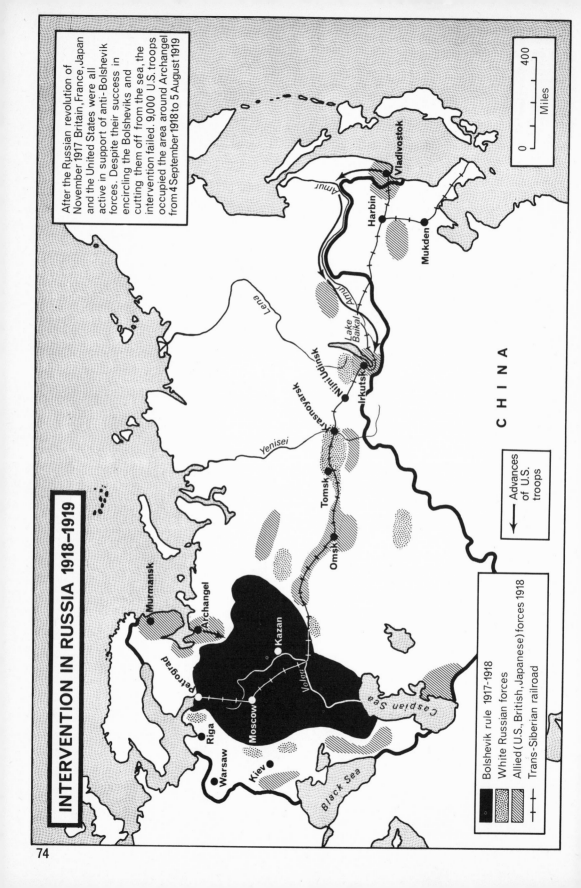

INTERVENTION IN RUSSIA 1918–1919

After the Russian revolution of November 1917 Britain, France, Japan and the United States were all active in support of anti-Bolshevik forces. Despite their success in encircling the Bolsheviks and cutting them off from the sea, the intervention failed. 9,000 U.S. troops occupied the area around Archangel from 4 September 1918 to 5 August 1919

400

0

Miles

Vladivostok

Harbin

Mukden

Amur

Amur

Lena

Lake Baikal

Irkutsk

Nijni Udinsk

Krasnoyarsk

C H I N A

Yenisei

Tomsk

Omsk

Murmansk

Archangel

Kazan

Petrograd

Volga

Riga

Moscow

Warsaw

Kiev

Caspian Sea

Black Sea

→ Advances of U.S. troops

■ Bolshevik rule 1917-1918

White Russian forces

Allied (U.S., British, Japanese) forces 1918

+ Trans-Siberian railroad

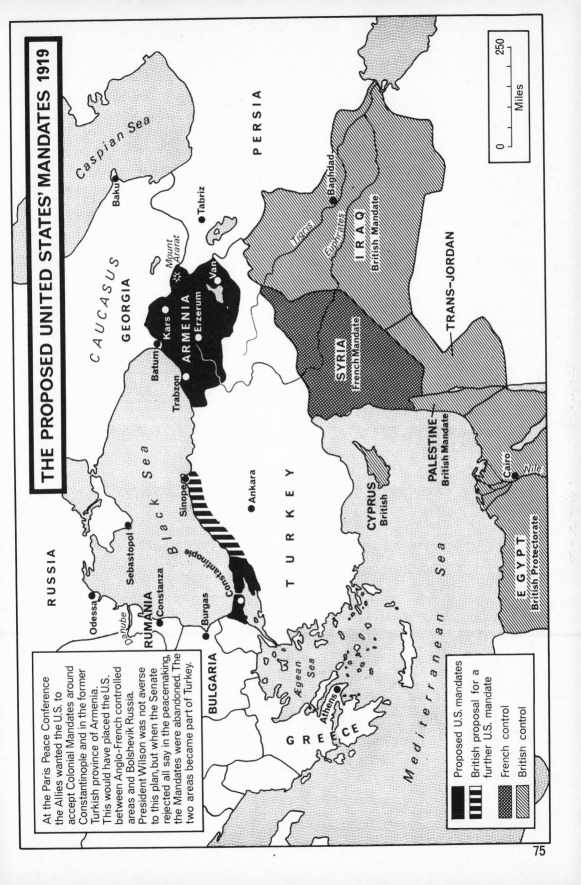

THE PROPOSED UNITED STATES' MANDATES 1919

At the Paris Peace Conference the Allies wanted the U.S. to accept Colonial Mandates around Constantinople and in the former Turkish province of Armenia. This would have placed the U.S. between Anglo-French controlled areas and Bolshevik Russia. President Wilson was not averse to this plan, but when the Senate rejected all say in the peacemaking, the Mandates were abandoned. The two areas became part of Turkey.

Proposed U.S. mandates

British proposal for a further U.S. mandate

French control

British control

RUSSIA

Odessa

Sebastopol

RUMANIA
Constanza

Danube

Burgas

BULGARIA

Black Sea

Sinope

Constantinople

GREECE
Athens

Aegean Sea

Mediterranean Sea

Caspian Sea

Baku

Tabriz

PERSIA

Mount Ararat

GEORGIA

CAUCASUS

Kars

ARMENIA
Erzerum

Van

Batum

Trabzon

TURKEY

Ankara

CYPRUS
British

SYRIA
French Mandate

IRAQ
British Mandate

Baghdad

Tigris

Euphrates

TRANS-JORDAN

PALESTINE
British Mandate

Cairo

Nile

EGYPT
British Protectorate

250

0

Miles

75

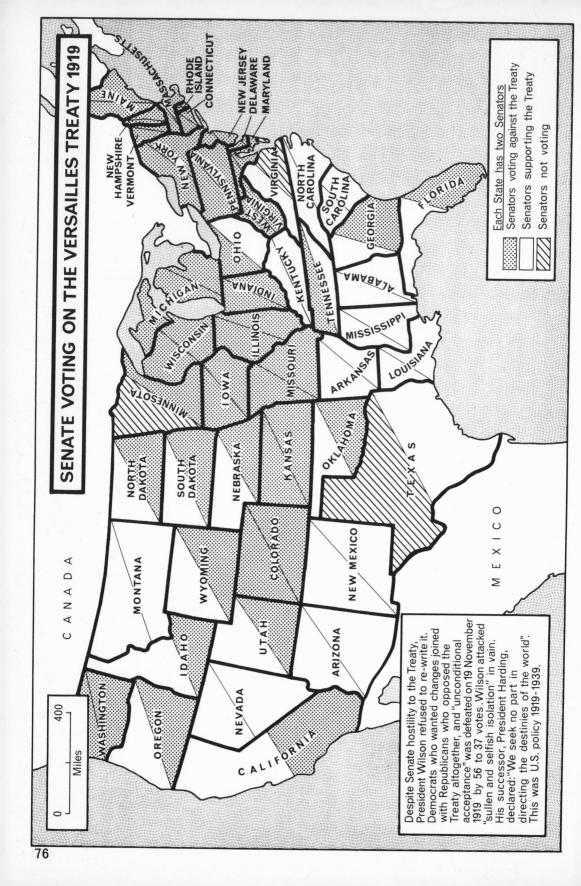

SENATE VOTING ON THE VERSAILLES TREATY 1919

Each State has two Senators

Senators voting against the Treaty

Senators supporting the Treaty

Senators not voting

Despite Senate hostility to the Treaty, President Wilson refused to re-write it. Democrats who wanted changes joined with Republicans who opposed the Treaty altogether, and "unconditional acceptance" was defeated on 19 November 1919 by 56 to 37 votes. Wilson attacked "sullen and selfish isolation" in vain. His successor, President Harding, declared: "We seek no part in directing the destinies of the world". This was U.S. policy 1919-1939.

CANADA

MEXICO

400

0

Miles

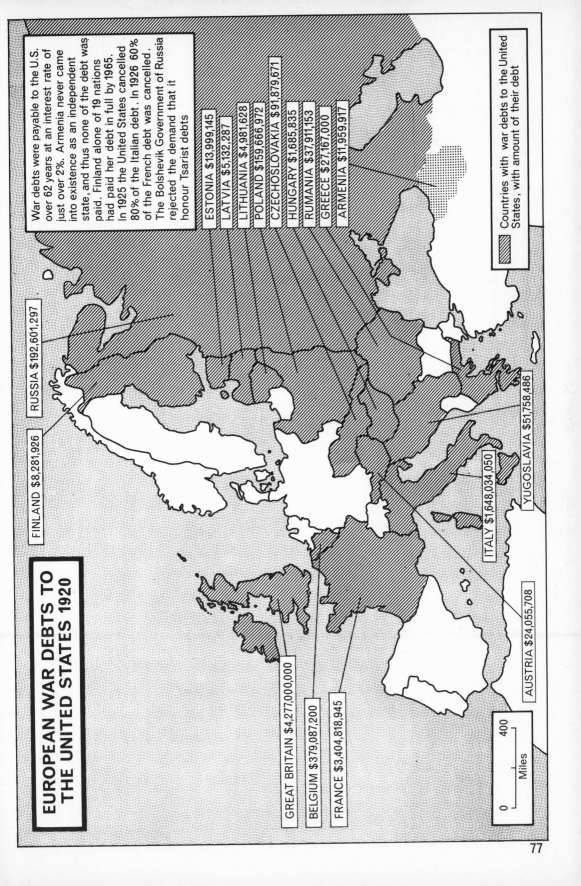

EUROPEAN WAR DEBTS TO THE UNITED STATES 1920

War debts were payable to the U.S. over 62 years at an interest rate of just over 2%. Armenia never came into existence as an independent state, and thus none of the debt was paid. Finland alone of 19 nations had paid her debt in full by 1965. In 1925 the United States cancelled 80% of the Italian debt. In 1926 60% of the French debt was cancelled. The Bolshevik Government of Russia rejected the demand that it honour Tsarist debts

ESTONIA $13,999,145
LATVIA $5,132,287
LITHUANIA $4,981,628
POLAND $159,666,972
CZECHOSLOVAKIA $91,879,671
HUNGARY $1,685,835
RUMANIA $37,911,153
GREECE $27,167,000
ARMENIA $11,959,917

RUSSIA $192,601,297

FINLAND $8,281,926

GREAT BRITAIN $4,277,000,000

BELGIUM $379,087,200

FRANCE $3,404,818,945

ITALY $1,648,034,050

YUGOSLAVIA $51,758,486

AUSTRIA $24,055,708

Countries with war debts to the United States, with amount of their debt

400

0

Miles

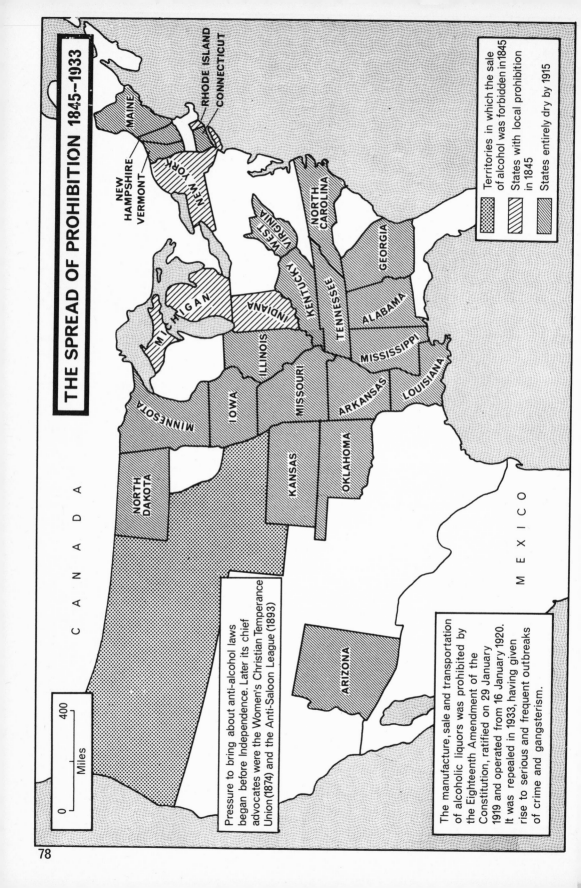

THE SPREAD OF PROHIBITION 1845-1933

CANADA

MEXICO

NEW HAMPSHIRE
VERMONT
MAINE
RHODE ISLAND
CONNECTICUT
NEW YORK
WEST VIRGINIA
NORTH CAROLINA
GEORGIA
MICHIGAN
INDIANA
KENTUCKY
TENNESSEE
ALABAMA
ILLINOIS
MISSISSIPPI
IOWA
MISSOURI
ARKANSAS
LOUISIANA
MINNESOTA
KANSAS
OKLAHOMA
NORTH DAKOTA
ARIZONA

Territories in which the sale
of alcohol was forbidden in1845

States with local prohibition
in 1845

States entirely dry by 1915

Pressure to bring about anti-alcohol laws
began before Independence. Later its chief
advocates were the Women's Christian Temperance
Union(1874) and the Anti-Saloon League (1893)

The manufacture, sale and transportation
of alcoholic liquors was prohibited by
the Eighteenth Amendment of the
Constitution, ratified on 29 January
1919 and operated from 16 January 1920.
It was repealed in 1933, having given
rise to serious and frequent outbreaks
of crime and gangsterism.

0   400
Miles

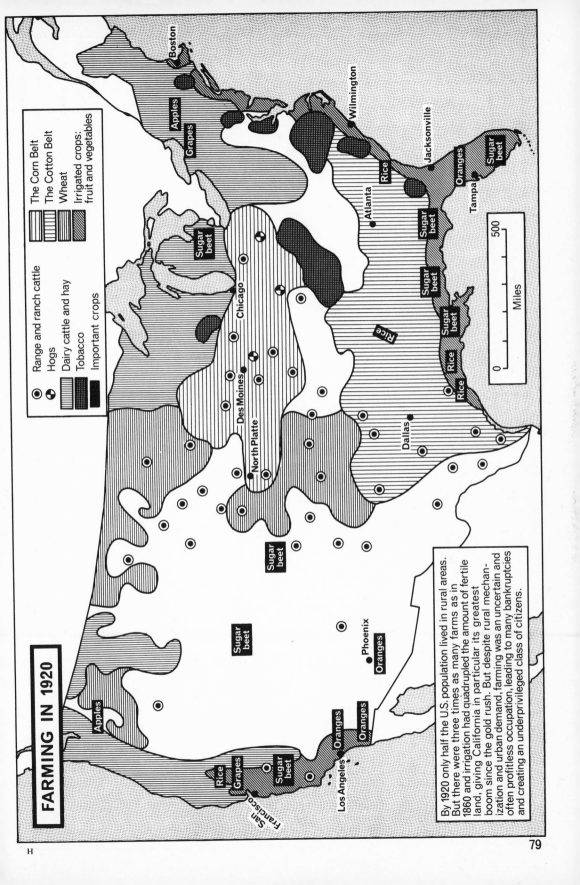

FARMING IN 1920

Range and ranch cattle
Hogs
Dairy cattle and hay
Tobacco
Important crops

The Corn Belt
The Cotton Belt
Wheat
Irrigated crops:
fruit and vegetables

Apples
Grapes
Boston
Wilmington
Sugar beet
Atlanta
Rice
Jacksonville
Sugar beet
Oranges
Tampa
Sugar beet
Sugar beet
Chicago
Rice
Sugar beet
Des Moines
Rice
North Platte
Rice
Rice
Dallas
Sugar beet
Sugar beet
Phoenix
Oranges
Apples
Oranges
Oranges
Rice
Grapes
Sugar beet
Los Angeles
San Francisco

0   500
Miles

By 1920 only half the U.S. population lived in rural areas.
But there were three times as many farms as in
1860 and irrigation had quadrupled the amount of fertile
land, giving California in particular its greatest
boom since the gold rush. But despite rural mechan-
ization and urban demand, farming was an uncertain and
often profitless occupation, leading to many bankruptcies
and creating an underprivileged class of citizens.

H

79

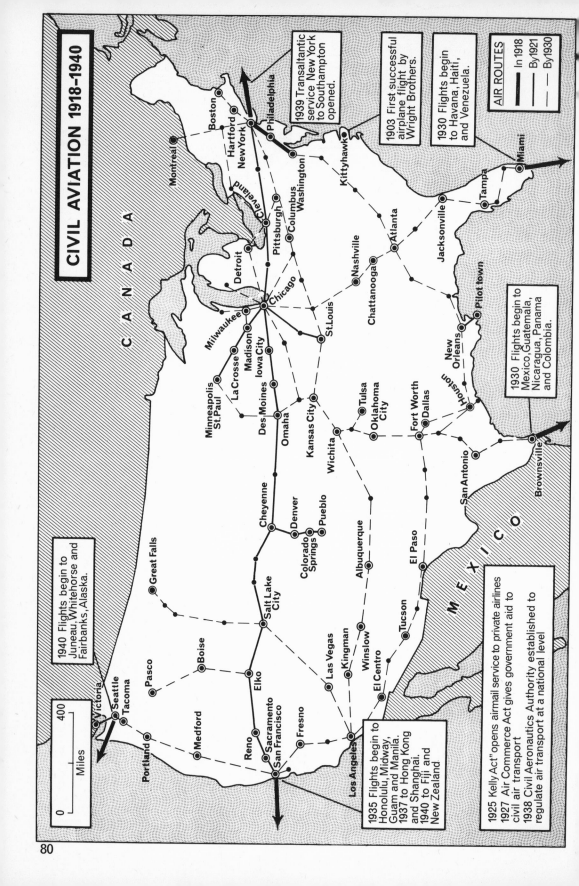

CIVIL AVIATION 1918–1940

CANADA

MEXICO

AIR ROUTES
- In 1918
- By 1921
- By 1930

1939 Transatlantic service New York to Southampton opened.

1903 First successful airplane flight by Wright Brothers.

1930 Flights begin to Havana, Haiti, and Venezuela.

1930 Flights begin to Mexico, Guatemala, Nicaragua, Panama and Colombia.

1940 Flights begin to Juneau, Whitehorse and Fairbanks, Alaska.

1925 Kelly Act opens airmail service to private airlines
1927 Air Commerce Act gives government aid to civil air transport
1938 Civil Aeronautics Authority established to regulate air transport at a national level

1935 Flights begin to Honolulu, Midway, Guam and Manila.
1937 to Hong Kong and Shanghai.
1940 to Fiji and New Zealand.

Cities
Boston, Hartford, New York, Philadelphia, Montreal, Cleveland, Columbus, Washington, Pittsburgh, Detroit, Kittyhawk, Atlanta, Jacksonville, Tampa, Miami, Chicago, Nashville, Chattanooga, St. Louis, Milwaukee, Madison, Iowa City, La Crosse, Minneapolis St. Paul, Des Moines, Omaha, Kansas City, Wichita, Tulsa, Oklahoma City, Fort Worth, Dallas, New Orleans, Pilot town, Houston, San Antonio, Brownsville, Cheyenne, Denver, Pueblo, Colorado Springs, Albuquerque, El Paso, Great Falls, Salt Lake City, Las Vegas, Kingman, Winslow, Tucson, El Centro, Boise, Pasco, Elko, Reno, Sacramento, San Francisco, Fresno, Medford, Portland, Victoria, Seattle, Tacoma, Los Angeles

Miles
0   400

80

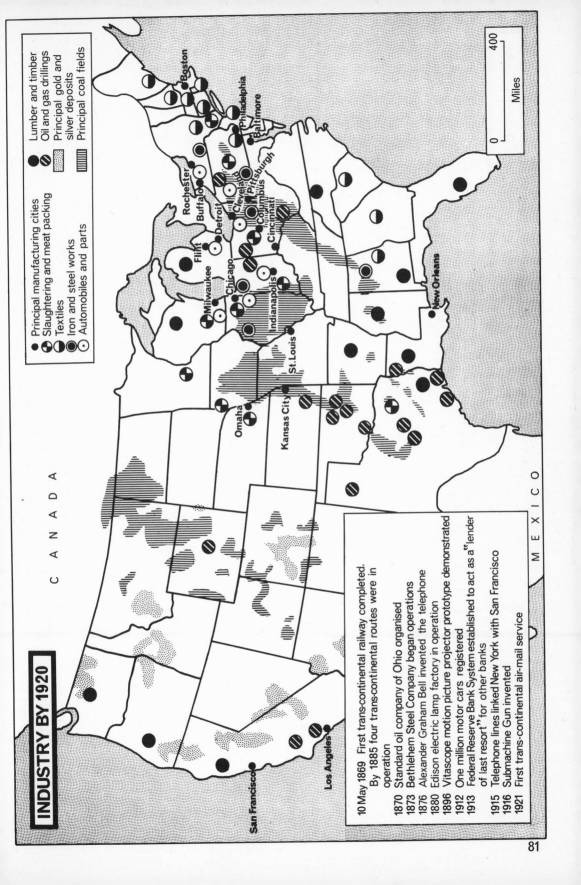

INDUSTRY BY 1920

Legend:
- Principal manufacturing cities
- Slaughtering and meat packing
- Textiles
- Iron and steel works
- Automobiles and parts

- Lumber and timber
- Oil and gas drillings
- Principal gold and silver deposits
- Principal coal fields

CANADA

MEXICO

Boston
Philadelphia
Baltimore
Pittsburgh
Rochester
Buffalo
Cleveland
Columbus
Detroit
Cincinnati
Flint
Chicago
Milwaukee
Indianapolis
St. Louis
Omaha
Kansas City
New Orleans
San Francisco
Los Angeles

0   400
Miles

10 May 1869 First trans-continental railway completed. By 1885 four trans-continental routes were in operation
1870 Standard oil company of Ohio organised
1873 Bethlehem Steel Company began operations
1876 Alexander Graham Bell invented the telephone
1880 Edison electric lamp factory in operation
1896 Vitascope motion picture projector prototype demonstrated
1912 One million motor cars registered
1913 Federal Reserve Bank System established to act as a "lender of last resort" for other banks
1915 Telephone lines linked New York with San Francisco
1916 Submachine Gun invented
1921 First trans-continental air-mail service

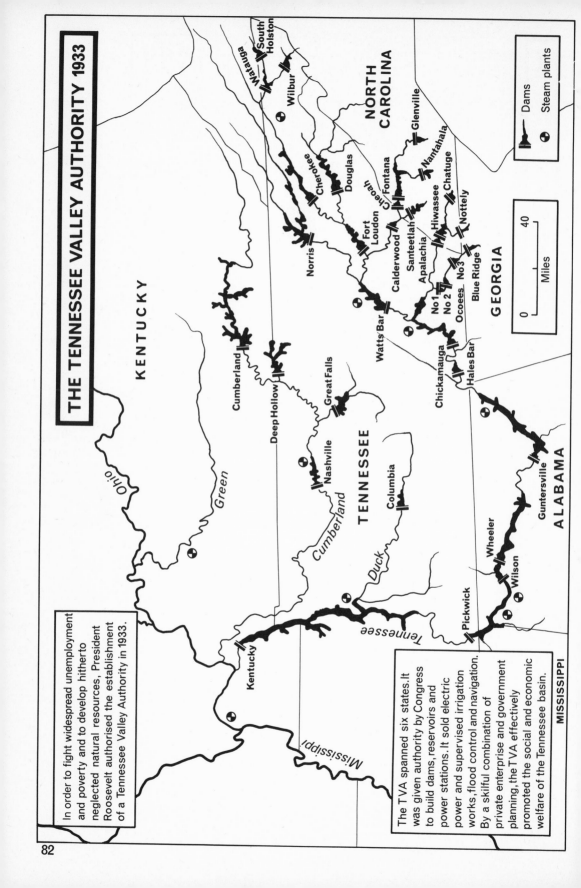

THE TENNESSEE VALLEY AUTHORITY 1933

In order to fight widespread unemployment and poverty and to develop hitherto neglected natural resources, President Roosevelt authorised the establishment of a Tennessee Valley Authority in 1933.

The TVA spanned six states. It was given authority by Congress to build dams, reservoirs and power stations. It sold electric power and supervised irrigation works, flood control and navigation. By a skilful combination of private enterprise and government planning, the TVA effectively promoted the social and economic welfare of the Tennessee basin.

Dams

Steam plants

0   40
Miles

KENTUCKY

TENNESSEE

NORTH CAROLINA

GEORGIA

ALABAMA

MISSISSIPPI

Ohio

Green

Cumberland

Duck

Tennessee

Mississippi

Watauga
South Holston
Wilbur
Glenville
Nantahala
Cherokee
Douglas
Chatuge
Cheoah
Fontana
Hiwassee
Nottely
Fort Loudon
Calderwood
Santeetlah
Apalachia
No 1
No 2
No 3
Ocoees
Blue Ridge
Norris
Watts Bar
Chickamauga
Hales Bar
Cumberland
Deep Hollow
Great Falls
Nashville
Columbia
Wheeler
Guntersville
Wilson
Pickwick
Kentucky

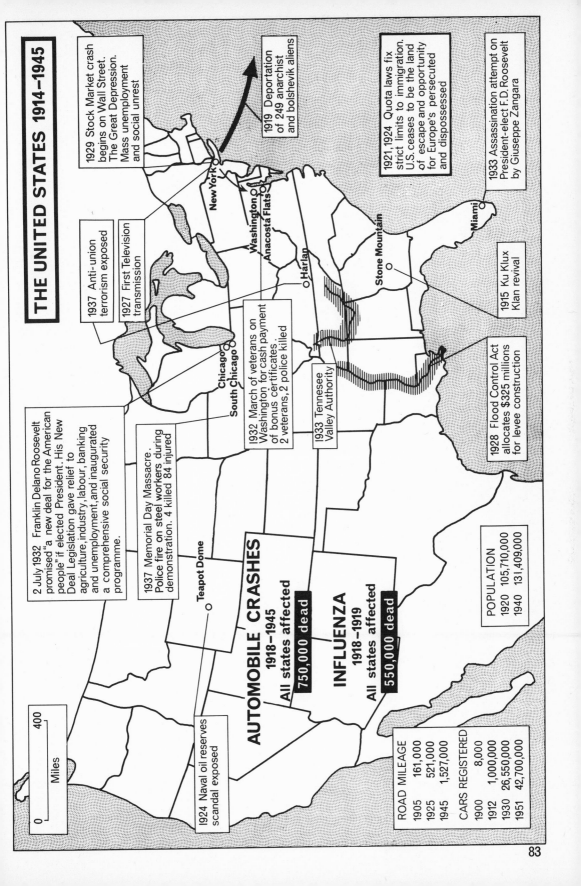

THE UNITED STATES 1914–1945

1929 Stock Market crash begins on Wall Street. The Great Depression. Mass unemployment and social unrest

1919 Deportation of 249 anarchist and bolshevik aliens

1921,1924 Quota laws fix strict limits to immigration. U.S. ceases to be the land of escape and opportunity for Europe's persecuted and dispossessed

1933 Assassination attempt on President-elect F.D. Roosevelt by Giuseppe Zangara

1937 Anti-union terrorism exposed

1927 First Television transmission

1915 Ku Klux Klan revival

2 July 1932 Franklin Delano Roosevelt promised "a new deal for the American people" if elected President. His New Deal Legislation gave relief to agriculture, industry, labour, banking and unemployment, and inaugurated a comprehensive social security programme.

1937 Memorial Day Massacre. Police fire on steel workers during demonstration. 4 killed 84 injured

1932 March of veterans on Washington for cash payment of bonus certificates. 2 veterans, 2 police killed

1933 Tennessee Valley Authority

1928 Flood Control Act allocates $325 millions for levee construction

New York

Washington
Anacosta Flats

Harlan

Stone Mountain

Miami

Chicago
South Chicago

Teapot Dome

AUTOMOBILE CRASHES
1918–1945
All states affected
750,000 dead

INFLUENZA
1918–1919
All states affected
550,000 dead

1924 Naval oil reserves scandal exposed

POPULATION	
1920	105,710,000
1940	131,409,000

ROAD MILEAGE	
1905	161,000
1925	521,000
1945	1,527,000

CARS REGISTERED	
1900	8,000
1912	1,000,000
1930	26,550,000
1951	42,700,000

Miles
0   400

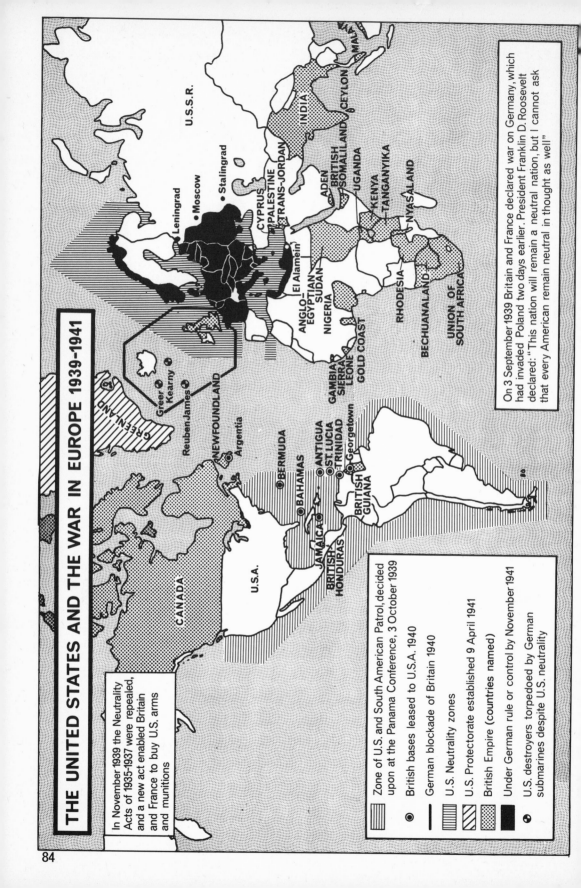

THE UNITED STATES AND THE WAR IN EUROPE 1939-1941

In November 1939 the Neutrality Acts of 1935-1937 were repealed, and a new act enabled Britain and France to buy U.S. arms and munitions

On 3 September 1939 Britain and France declared war on Germany, which had invaded Poland two days earlier. President Franklin D. Roosevelt declared: "This nation will remain a neutral nation, but I cannot ask that every American remain neutral in thought as well"

Zone of U.S. and South American Patrol, decided upon at the Panama Conference, 3 October 1939

British bases leased to U.S.A. 1940

German blockade of Britain 1940

U.S. Neutrality zones

U.S. Protectorate established 9 April 1941

British Empire (countries named)

Under German rule or control by November 1941

U.S. destroyers torpedoed by German submarines despite U.S. neutrality

U.S.S.R.

Leningrad
Moscow • Stalingrad

INDIA
CYPRUS
PALESTINE
TRANS-JORDAN
ADEN
BRITISH SOMALILAND
CEYLON
UGANDA
KENYA
TANGANYIKA
NYASALAND
[El Alamein]
ANGLO-EGYPTIAN SUDAN
NIGERIA
RHODESIA
BECHUANALAND
UNION OF SOUTH AFRICA
GOLD COAST
SIERRA LEONE
GAMBIA

GREENLAND
Greer
(Kearny)
Reuben James
NEWFOUNDLAND
Argentia

CANADA

U.S.A.

BERMUDA
BAHAMAS
JAMAICA
BRITISH HONDURAS
ANTIGUA
ST LUCIA
TRINIDAD
Georgetown
BRITISH GUIANA

84

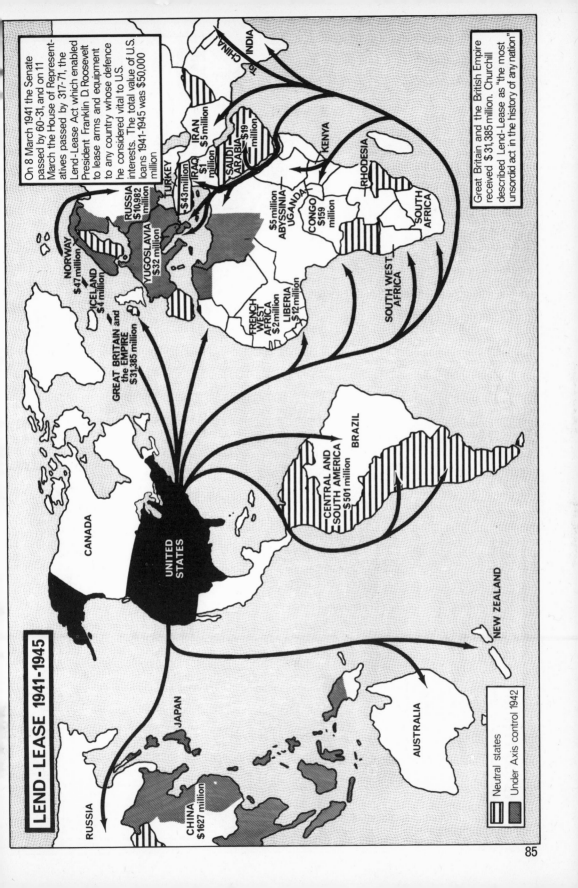

LEND-LEASE 1941-1945

On 8 March 1941 the Senate passed by 60-31, and on 11 March the House of Representatives passed by 317-71, the Lend-Lease Act which enabled President Franklin D Roosevelt to lease arms and equipment to any country whose defence he considered vital to U.S. interests. The total value of U.S. loans 1941-1945 was $50,000 million

Great Britain and the British Empire received $31,385 million. Churchill described Lend-Lease as "the most unsordid act in the history of any nation"

RUSSIA $10,982 million

NORWAY $47 million

ICELAND $4 million

YUGOSLAVIA $32 million

TURKEY $43 million

IRAQ $1 million

IRAN $5 million

SAUDI ARABIA $19 million

To CHINA

INDIA

KENYA

RHODESIA

ABYSSINIA UGANDA $5 million

CONGO $159 million

SOUTH AFRICA

FRENCH WEST AFRICA $2 million

LIBERIA $12 million

SOUTH WEST AFRICA

GREAT BRITAIN and the EMPIRE $31,385 million

CANADA

UNITED STATES

CENTRAL AND SOUTH AMERICA $501 million

BRAZIL

NEW ZEALAND

AUSTRALIA

JAPAN

RUSSIA

CHINA $1627 million

Neutral states

Under Axis control 1942

85

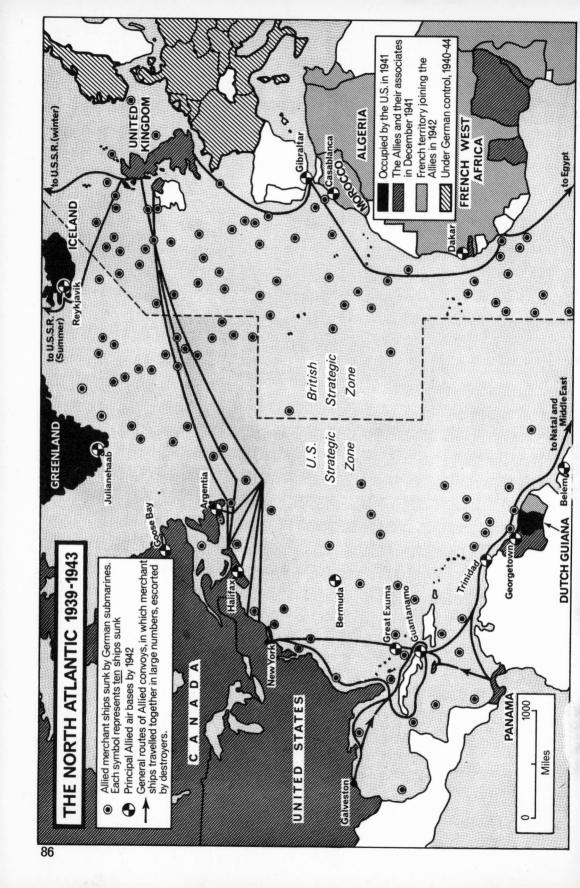

THE NORTH ATLANTIC 1939-1943

⊙ Allied merchant ships sunk by German submarines.
  Each symbol represents <u>ten</u> ships sunk

◕ Principal Allied air bases by 1942

↑ General routes of Allied convoys, in which merchant
  ships travelled together in large numbers, escorted
  by destroyers.

Occupied by the U.S. in 1941

The Allies and their associates
in December 1941

French territory joining the
Allies in 1942

Under German control, 1940-44

GREENLAND

ICELAND

Reykjavik

to U.S.S.R.
(Summer)

to U.S.S.R. (winter)

UNITED
KINGDOM

Gibraltar

Casablanca

MOROCCO

ALGERIA

FRENCH WEST
AFRICA

Dakar

to Egypt

Julianehaab

Goose Bay

Argentia

Halifax

CANADA

UNITED STATES

New York

Galveston

PANAMA

Bermuda

Great Exuma

Guantanamo

Trinidad

Georgetown

DUTCH GUIANA

Belem

to Natal and
Middle East

U.S.
Strategic
Zone

British
Strategic
Zone

Miles

0   1000

86

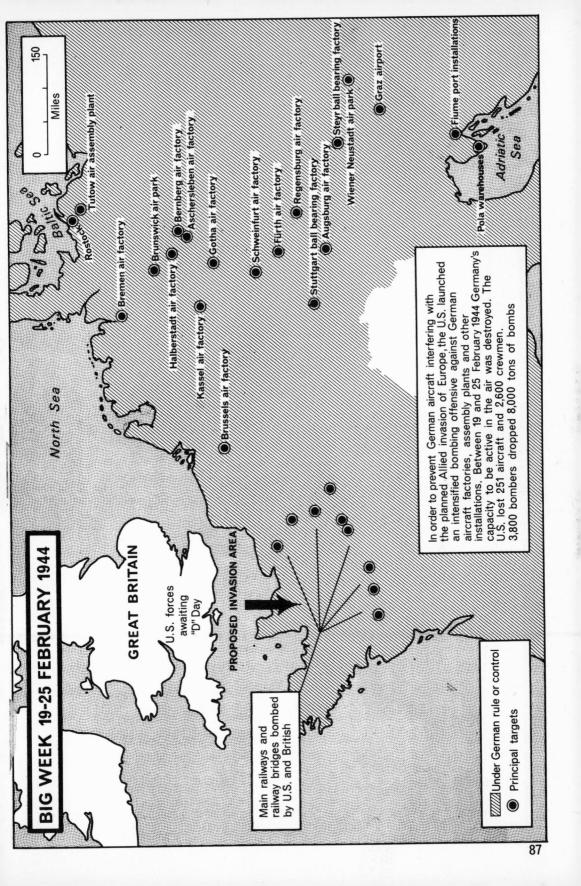

BIG WEEK 19-25 FEBRUARY 1944

150

0

Miles

Baltic Sea

North Sea

GREAT BRITAIN

U.S. forces awaiting "D" Day

PROPOSED INVASION AREA

Tutow air assembly plant

Rostock

Bremen air factory

Brunswick air park

Halberstadt air factory

Bernberg air factory
Aschersleben air factory

Gotha air factory

Kassel air factory

Schweinfurt air factory

Fürth air factory

Regensburg air factory

Stuttgart ball bearing factory

Augsburg air factory

Steyr ball bearing factory

Wiener Neustadt air park

Graz airport

Fiume port installations

Pola warehouses

Adriatic Sea

Brussels air factory

In order to prevent German aircraft interfering with the planned Allied invasion of Europe, the U.S. launched an intensified bombing offensive against German aircraft factories, assembly plants and other installations. Between 19 and 25 February 1944 Germany's capacity to be active in the air was destroyed. The U.S. lost 251 aircraft and 2,600 crewmen; 3,800 bombers dropped 8,000 tons of bombs

Main railways and railway bridges bombed by U.S. and British

Under German rule or control

Principal targets

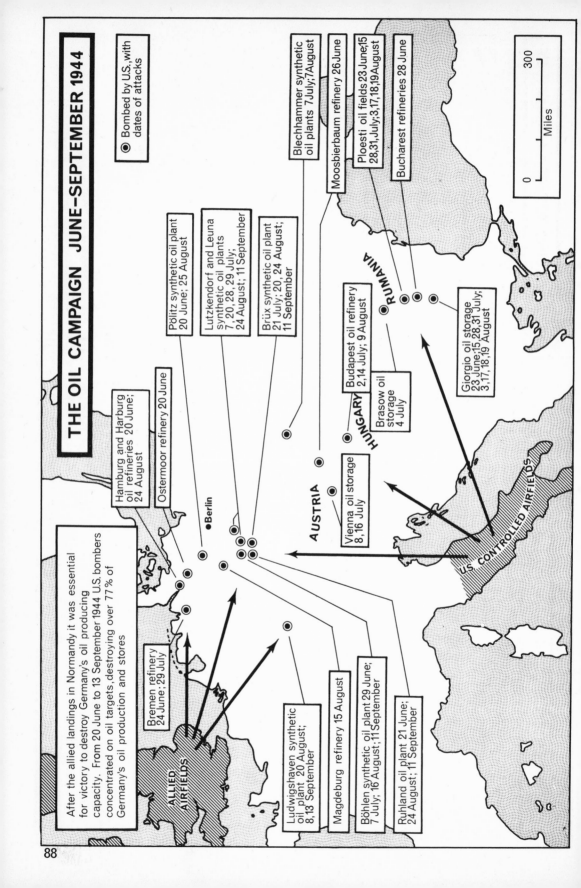

THE OIL CAMPAIGN JUNE–SEPTEMBER 1944

⊙ Bombed by U.S. with dates of attacks

0 — 300
Miles

After the allied landings in Normandy it was essential for victory to destroy Germany's oil producing capacity. From 20 June to 13 September 1944 U.S. bombers concentrated on oil targets, destroying over 77% of Germany's oil production and stores

Blechhammer synthetic oil plants 7 July; 7 August

Moosbierbaum refinery 26 June

Ploesti oil fields 23 June;15 28,31,July;3,17,18,19August

Bucharest refineries 28 June

Pölitz synthetic oil plant 20 June; 25 August

Lutzkendorf and Leuna synthetic oil plants 7, 20, 28, 29 July; 24 August; 11 September

Brüx synthetic oil plant 21 July; 20, 24 August; 11 September

Hamburg and Harburg oil refineries 20 June; 24 August

Ostermoor refinery 20 June

Budapest oil refinery 2, 14 July; 9 August

Brasow oil storage 4 July

Giorgio oil storage 23 June;15,28,31 July; 3,17,18,19 August

Vienna oil storage 8, 16 July

RUMANIA

HUNGARY

AUSTRIA

●Berlin

U.S. CONTROLLED AIRFIELDS

ALLIED AIRFIELDS

Bremen refinery 24 June; 29 July

Ludwigshaven synthetic oil plant 20 August; 8, 13 September

Magdeburg refinery 15 August

Böhlen synthetic oil plant 29 June; 7 July; 16 August; 11September

Ruhland oil plant 21 June; 24 August; 11 September

88

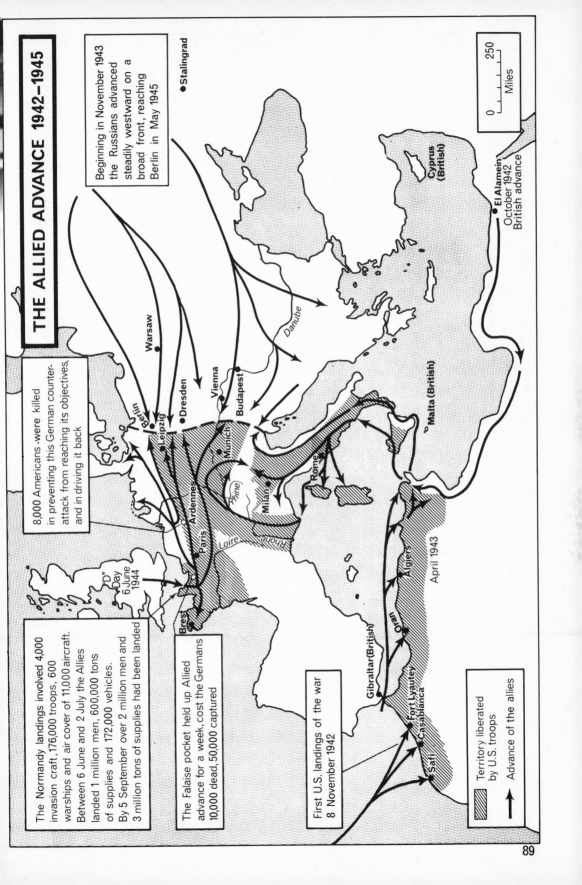

THE ALLIED ADVANCE 1942-1945

Beginning in November 1943 the Russians advanced steadily westward on a broad front, reaching Berlin in May 1945

• Stalingrad

8,000 Americans -were killed in preventing this German counter-attack from reaching its objectives, and in driving it back

The Normandy landings involved 4,000 invasion craft, 176,000 troops, 600 warships and air cover of 11,000 aircraft. Between 6 June and 2 July the Allies landed 1 million men, 600,000 tons of supplies and 172,000 vehicles. By 5 September over 2 million men and 3 million tons of supplies had been landed

The Falaise pocket held up Allied advance for a week, cost the Germans 10,000 dead, 50,000 captured

First U.S. landings of the war 8 November 1942

"D" Day 6 June 1944

Brest

Paris

Ardennes

Loire

Rhine

Rhône

Garonne

Berlin

Leipzig

• Dresden

Warsaw

Vienna

Budapest

Munich

Milan

Rome

Danube

Malta (British)

Cyprus (British)

• El Alamein
October 1942
British advance

Gibraltar (British)

Oran

Algiers

Fort Lyautey
Casablanca

Safi

April 1943

Territory liberated by U.S. troops

Advance of the allies

0   250
Miles

89

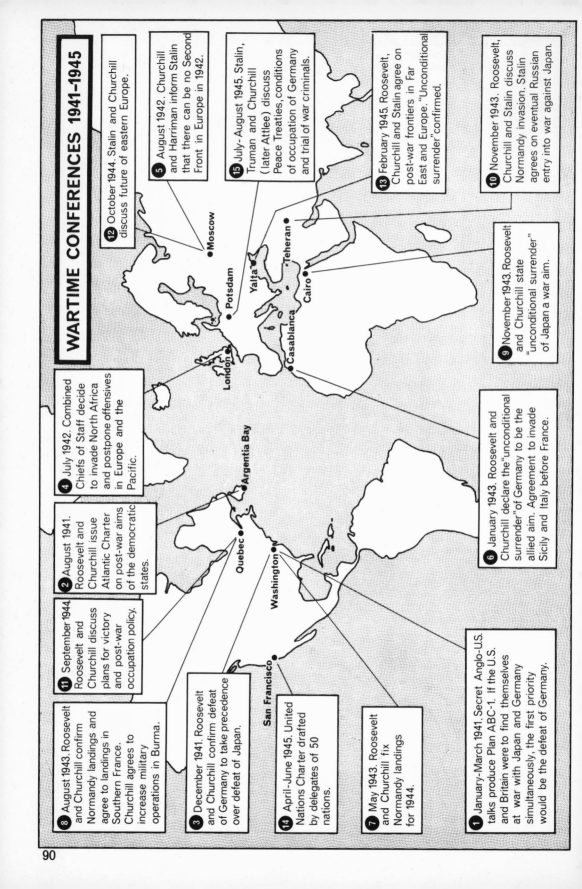

WARTIME CONFERENCES 1941-1945

12 October 1944. Stalin and Churchill discuss future of eastern Europe.

5 August 1942. Churchill and Harriman inform Stalin that there can be no Second Front in Europe in 1942.

15 July-August 1945. Stalin, Truman and Churchill (later Attlee) discuss Peace Treaties, conditions of occupation of Germany and trial of war criminals.

13 February 1945. Roosevelt, Churchill and Stalin agree on post-war frontiers in Far East and Europe. "Unconditional surrender" confirmed.

10 November 1943. Roosevelt, Churchill and Stalin discuss Normandy invasion. Stalin agrees on eventual Russian entry into war against Japan.

9 November 1943. Roosevelt and Churchill state "unconditional surrender" of Japan a war aim.

4 July 1942. Combined Chiefs of Staff decide to invade North Africa and postpone offensives in Europe and the Pacific.

2 August 1941. Roosevelt and Churchill issue Atlantic Charter on post-war aims of the democratic states.

11 September 1944. Roosevelt and Churchill discuss plans for victory and post-war occupation policy.

3 December 1941. Roosevelt and Churchill confirm defeat of Germany to take precedence over defeat of Japan.

14 April-June 1945. United Nations Charter drafted by delegates of 50 nations.

7 May 1943. Roosevelt and Churchill fix Normandy landings for 1944.

8 August 1943. Roosevelt and Churchill confirm Normandy landings and agree to landings in Southern France. Churchill agrees to increase military operations in Burma.

6 January 1943. Roosevelt and Churchill declare the "unconditional surrender" of Germany to be the allied aim. Agreement to invade Sicily and Italy before France.

1 January-March 1941. Secret Anglo-U.S. talks produce Plan ABC-1. If the U.S. and Britain were to find themselves at war with Japan and Germany simultaneously, the first priority would be the defeat of Germany.

Moscow

Potsdam

Yalta

Teheran

Casablanca

Cairo

London

Argentia Bay

Quebec

Washington

San Francisco

90

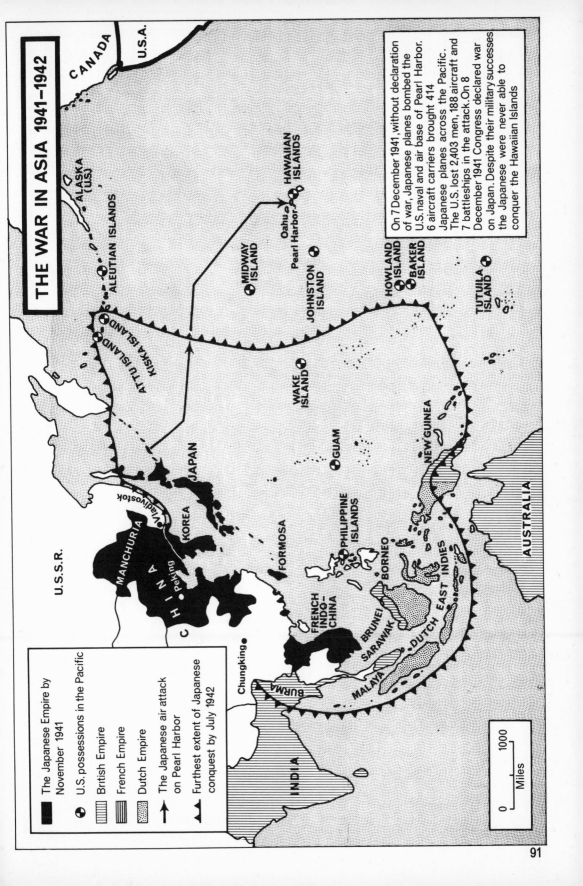

THE WAR IN ASIA 1941–1942

On 7 December 1941, without declaration of war, Japanese planes bombed the U.S. naval and air base of Pearl Harbor. 6 aircraft carriers brought 414 Japanese planes across the Pacific. The U.S. lost 2,403 men, 188 aircraft and 7 battleships in the attack. On 8 December 1941 Congress declared war on Japan. Despite their military successes the Japanese were never able to conquer the Hawaiian Islands.

CANADA

U.S.A.

ALASKA (U.S)

ALEUTIAN ISLANDS

HAWAIIAN ISLANDS

Oahu
Pearl Harbor

MIDWAY ISLAND

JOHNSTON ISLAND

HOWLAND ISLAND

BAKER ISLAND

TUTUILA ISLAND

ATTU ISLAND

KISKA ISLAND

WAKE ISLAND

GUAM

NEW GUINEA

JAPAN

Vladivostok

KOREA

FORMOSA

PHILIPPINE ISLANDS

BORNEO

BRUNEI

SARAWAK

DUTCH EAST INDIES

AUSTRALIA

MANCHURIA

C H I N A

Peking

FRENCH INDO-CHINA

MALAYA

BURMA

Chungking

INDIA

U.S.S.R.

Legend

■ The Japanese Empire by November 1941

⊕ U.S. possessions in the Pacific

▤ British Empire

▥ French Empire

⣿ Dutch Empire

↑ The Japanese air attack on Pearl Harbor

⊿ Furthest extent of Japanese conquest by July 1942

0   1000
Miles

91

THE DEFEAT OF JAPAN 1942–1945

On 26 July 1945 the Allies demanded Japan's surrender. Although some 400,000 Japanese civilians had been killed, the Japanese Government refused to surrender. On 6 August the U.S. dropped an atomic bomb on Hiroshima, killing 40,000 civilians. On 8 August Russia declared war on Japan. On 9 August the U.S. dropped a second atomic bomb on Nagasaki, killing 75,000 civilians. Japan surrendered on 14 August and U.S. troops began the occupation of Japan

On 9 March 1945, 234 bombers from Iwo Jima dropped 1,667 tons of incendiary bombs on Tokyo, Kawasaki and Yokohama, burning out 16 square miles of residential areas and killing over 80,000 people.

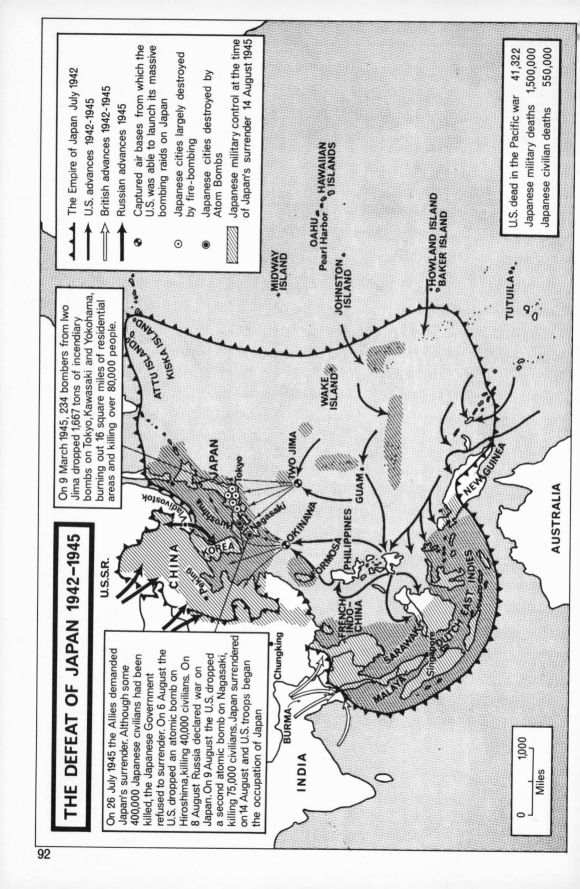

Key	
The Empire of Japan July 1942	
U.S. advances 1942-1945	
British advances 1942-1945	
Russian advances 1945	
Captured air bases from which the U.S. was able to launch its massive bombing raids on Japan	
Japanese cities largely destroyed by fire-bombing	
Japanese cities destroyed by Atom Bombs	
Japanese military control at the time of Japan's surrender 14 August 1945	

U.S. dead in the Pacific war	41,322
Japanese military deaths	1,500,000
Japanese civilian deaths	550,000

0   1,000

Miles

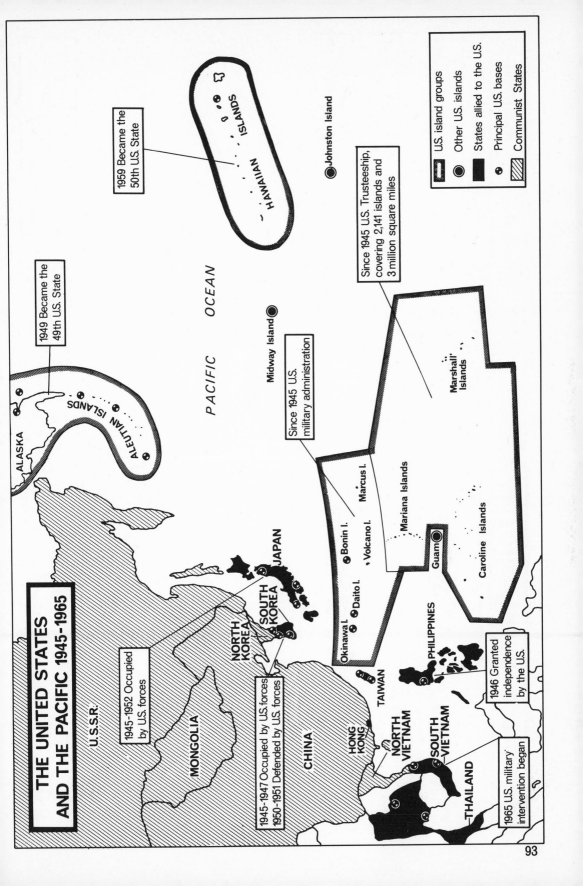

THE UNITED STATES
AND THE PACIFIC 1945-1965

U.S.S.R.

ALASKA

1949 Became the
49th U.S. State

ALEUTIAN ISLANDS

PACIFIC OCEAN

1959 Became the
50th U.S. State

HAWAIIAN ISLANDS

Johnston Island

Midway Island

Since 1945 U.S.
military administration

Since 1945 U.S. Trusteeship,
covering 2,141 islands and
3 million square miles

Marshall Islands

Marcus I.

Bonin I.

Volcano I.

Mariana Islands

Caroline Islands

Guam

Okinawa I.

Daito I.

MONGOLIA

CHINA

1945-1952 Occupied
by U.S. forces

JAPAN

SOUTH KOREA

NORTH KOREA

1945-1947 Occupied by U.S. forces
1950-1951 Defended by U.S. forces

HONG KONG

TAIWAN

PHILIPPINES

1946 Granted
independence by the U.S.

NORTH VIETNAM

SOUTH VIETNAM

THAILAND

1965 U.S. military
intervention began

U.S. island groups

Other U.S. islands

States allied to the U.S.

Principal U.S. bases

Communist States

93

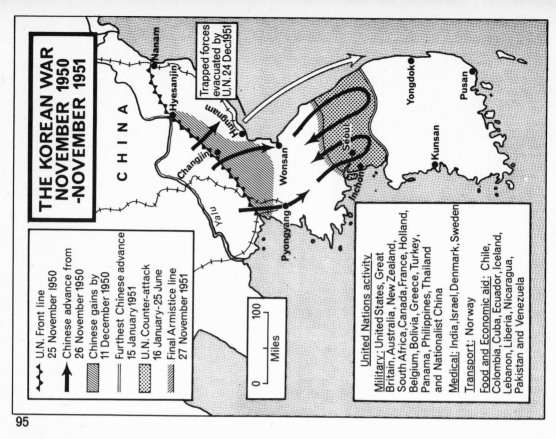

THE KOREAN WAR NOVEMBER 1950 -NOVEMBER 1951

Legend:
- U.N. Front line 25 November 1950
- Chinese advance from 26 November 1950
- Chinese gains by 11 December 1950
- Furthest Chinese advance 15 January 1951
- U.N. Counter-attack 16 January-25 June
- Final Armistice line 27 November 1951

Miles 0 — 100

Trapped forces evacuated by U.N. 24 Dec.1951

Map labels: CHINA, Yalu, Nanam, Hyesanjin, Hungnam, Changjin, Wonsan, Pyongyang, Inchon, Seoul, Yongdok, Kunsan, Pusan

United Nations activity

Military: United States, Great Britain, Australia, New Zealand, South Africa, Canada, France, Holland, Belgium, Bolivia, Greece, Turkey, Panama, Philippines, Thailand and Nationalist China

Medical: India, Israel, Denmark, Sweden

Transport: Norway

Food and Economic aid: Chile, Colombia, Cuba, Ecuador, Iceland, Lebanon, Liberia, Nicaragua, Pakistan and Venezuela

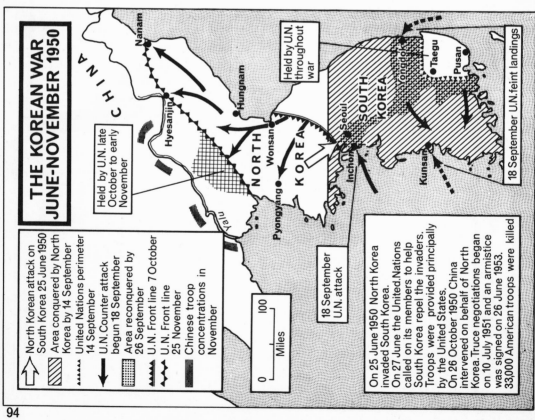

THE KOREAN WAR JUNE-NOVEMBER 1950

Legend:
- North Korean attack on South Korea 25 June 1950
- Area conquered by North Korea by 14 September
- United Nations perimeter 14 September
- U.N. Counter attack begun 18 September
- Area reconquered by 26 September
- U.N. Front line 7 October
- U.N. Front line 25 November
- Chinese troop concentrations in November

Miles 0 — 100

Held by U.N. late October to early November

Held by U.N. throughout war

18 September U.N. attack

18 September U.N. feint landings

Map labels: CHINA, Yalu, Nanam, Hyesanjin, Hungnam, Wonsan, Pyongyang, NORTH KOREA, Inchon, Seoul, SOUTH KOREA, Kunsan, Taegu, Yongdok, Pusan

On 25 June 1950 North Korea invaded South Korea.
On 27 June the United.Nations called on its members to help South Korea repel the invaders. Troops were provided principally by the United States.
On 26 October 1950 China intervened on behalf of North Korea. Truce negotiations began on 10 July 1951 and an armistice was signed on 26 June 1953. 33,000 American troops were killed

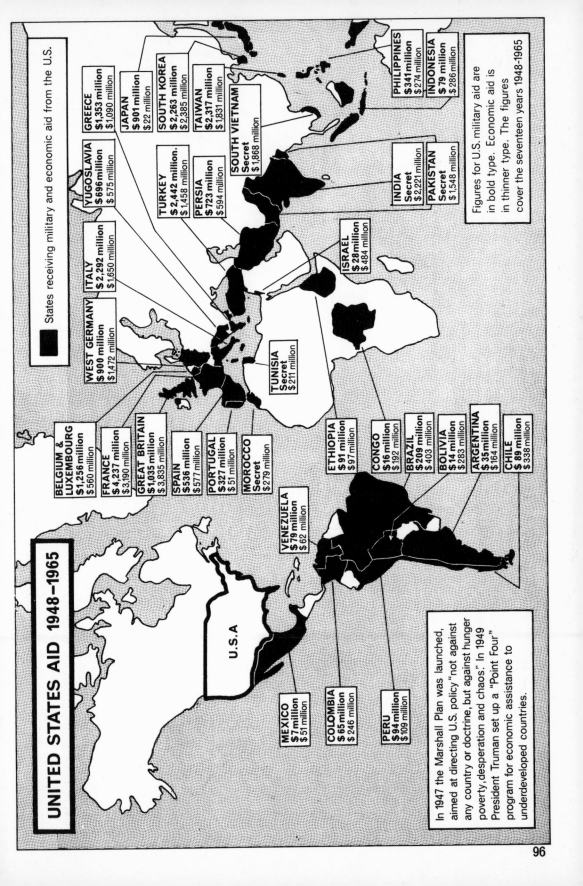

UNITED STATES AID 1948–1965

U.S.A

■ States receiving military and economic aid from the U.S.

BELGIUM & LUXEMBOURG
$1,256 million
$560 million

FRANCE
$4,237 million
$3,190 million

GREAT BRITAIN
$1,035 million
$3,835 million

SPAIN
$536 million
$577 million

PORTUGAL
$327 million
$51 million

MOROCCO
Secret
$279 million

WEST GERMANY
$900 million
$1,472 million

ITALY
$2,292 million
$1,650 million

YUGOSLAVIA
$696 million
$575 million

GREECE
$1,353 million
$1,090 million

JAPAN
$901 million
$22 million

SOUTH KOREA
$2,263 million
$2,385 million

TAIWAN
$2,317 million
$1,831 million

SOUTH VIETNAM
Secret
$1,868 million

TURKEY
$2,442 million.
$1,458 million

PERSIA
$723 million
$594 million

TUNISIA
Secret
$211 million

ISRAEL
$28 million
$484 million

INDIA
Secret
$2,221 million

PAKISTAN
Secret
$1,548 million

PHILIPPINES
$341 million
$274 million

INDONESIA
$79 million
$286 million

ETHIOPIA
$91 million
$97 million

CONGO
$16 million
$192 million

BRAZIL
$209 million
$403 million

BOLIVIA
$14 million
$283 million

ARGENTINA
$35 million
$164 million

CHILE
$89 million
$338 million

VENEZUELA
$79 million
$62 million

MEXICO
$7 million
$51 million

COLOMBIA
$65 million
$246 million

PERU
$94 million
$109 million

Figures for U.S. military aid are in bold type. Economic aid is in thinner type. The figures cover the seventeen years 1948-1965

In 1947 the Marshall Plan was launched, aimed at directing U.S. policy "not against any country or doctrine, but against hunger poverty, desperation and chaos." In 1949 President Truman set up a "Point Four" program for economic assistance to underdeveloped countries.

96

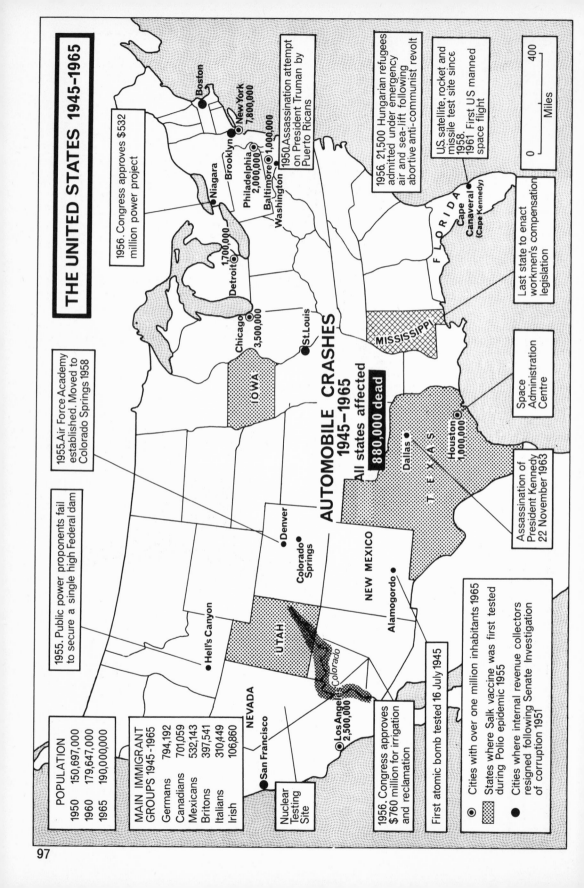

THE UNITED STATES 1945-1965

1956. Congress approves $532 million power project

1950. Assassination attempt on President Truman by Puerto Ricans

1956. 21,500 Hungarian refugees admitted under emergency air and sea-lift following abortive anti-communist revolt

U.S. satellite, rocket and missile test site since 1958. 1961 First US manned space flight

Last state to enact workmen's compensation legislation

Space Administration Centre

Assassination of President Kennedy 22 November 1963

1955. Air Force Academy established. Moved to Colorado Springs 1958

1955. Public power proponents fail to secure a single high Federal dam

0   400
Miles

Boston

New York 7,800,000

Brooklyn

Niagara

Philadelphia 2,000,000

Baltimore 1,000,000

Washington

Detroit 1,700,000

Chicago 3,500,000

St.Louis

Cape Canaveral (Cape Kennedy)

FLORIDA

MISSISSIPPI

IOWA

AUTOMOBILE CRASHES 1945-1965
All states affected
880,000 dead

Dallas

Houston 1,000,000

T E X A S

Denver

Colorado Springs

NEW MEXICO

Alamogordo

UTAH

Colorado

Hell's Canyon

NEVADA

Los Angeles 2,500,000

San Francisco

Nuclear Testing Site

1956. Congress approves $760 million for irrigation and reclamation

First atomic bomb tested 16 July 1945

POPULATION	
1950	150,697,000
1960	179,647,000
1965	190,000,000

MAIN IMMIGRANT GROUPS 1945-1965	
Germans	794,192
Canadians	701,059
Mexicans	532,143
Britons	397,541
Italians	310,449
Irish	106,860

⊙ Cities with over one million inhabitants 1965

States where Salk vaccine was first tested during Polio epidemic 1955

● Cities where internal revenue collectors resigned following Senate Investigation of corruption 1951

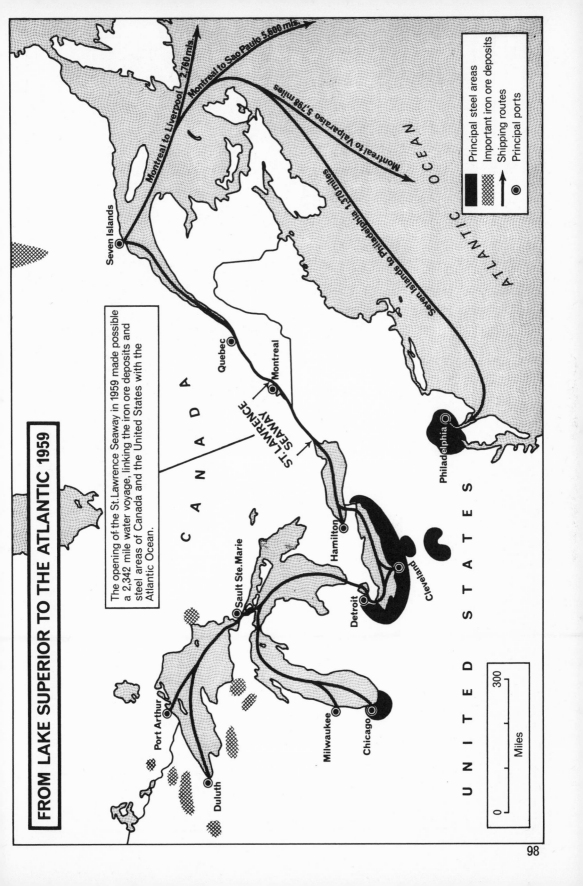

FROM LAKE SUPERIOR TO THE ATLANTIC 1959

The opening of the St. Lawrence Seaway in 1959 made possible a 2,342 mile water voyage, linking the iron ore deposits and steel areas of Canada and the United States with the Atlantic Ocean.

Montreal to Liverpool 2,760 mls.

Montreal to Sao Paulo 5,600 mls.

Montreal to Valparaiso 5,798 miles

Seven Islands to Philadelphia 1,310 miles

ST. LAWRENCE SEAWAY

ATLANTIC OCEAN

Principal steel areas
Important iron ore deposits
Shipping routes
Principal ports

Seven Islands

Quebec

Montreal

Hamilton

Sault Ste. Marie

Detroit

Cleveland

Philadelphia

Port Arthur

Duluth

Milwaukee

Chicago

CANADA

UNITED STATES

0   Miles   300

98

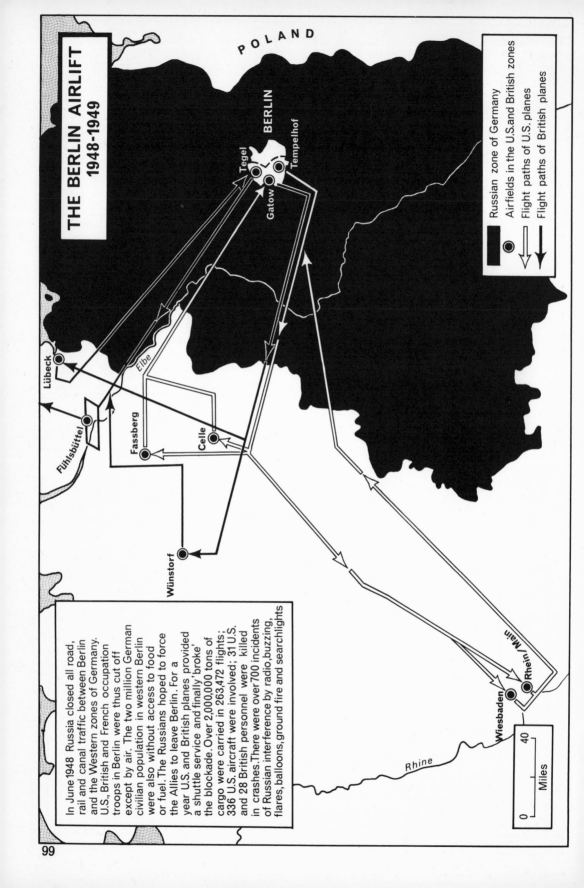

99

POLAND

THE BERLIN AIRLIFT 1948-1949

BERLIN

Tegel
Gatow
Tempelhof

Lübeck

Fühlsbüttel

Fassberg

Celle

Elbe

Wünstorf

Wiesbaden

Rhein / Main

Rhine

Russian zone of Germany

⊙ Airfields in the U.S.and British zones

⇨ Flight paths of U.S. planes

→ Flight paths of British planes

In June 1948 Russia closed all road, rail and canal traffic between Berlin and the Western zones of Germany. U.S., British and French occupation troops in Berlin were thus cut off except by air. The two million German civilian population in western Berlin were also without access to food or fuel. The Russians hoped to force the Allies to leave Berlin. For a year U.S. and British planes provided a shuttle service and finally 'broke' the blockade. Over 2,000,000 tons of cargo were carried in 263,472 flights; 336 U.S. aircraft were involved; 31 U.S. and 28 British personnel were killed in crashes. There were over 700 incidents of Russian interference by radio, buzzing, flares, balloons, ground fire and searchlights

0   40

Miles

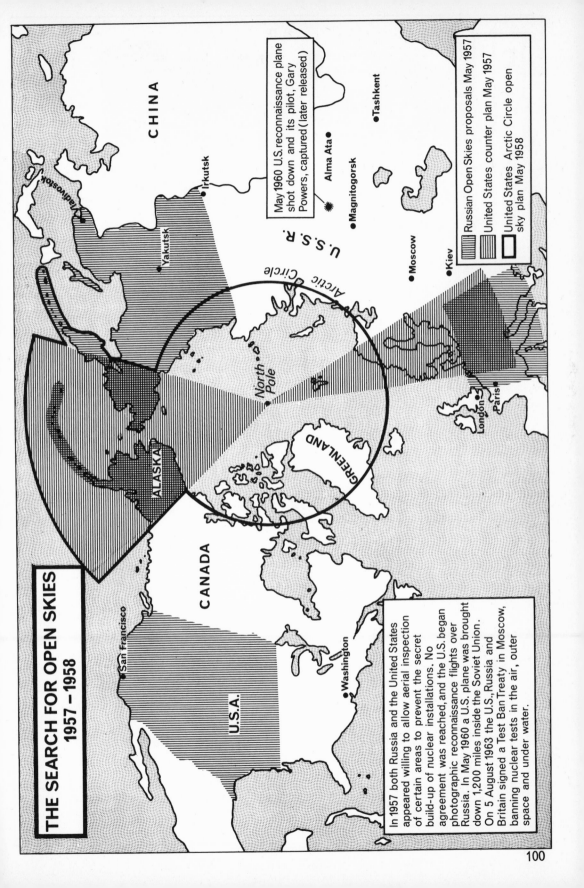

THE SEARCH FOR OPEN SKIES
1957 – 1958

CHINA

U.S.S.R.

Vladivostok

Irkutsk

Yakutsk

Alma Ata

Magnitogorsk

Tashkent

Moscow

Kiev

May 1960 U.S. reconnaissance plane shot down and its pilot, Gary Powers, captured (later released)

Russian Open Skies proposals May 1957

United States counter plan May 1957

United States Arctic Circle open sky plan May 1958

Arctic Circle

North Pole

GREENLAND

ALASKA

CANADA

U.S.A.

San Francisco

Washington

London

Paris

In 1957 both Russia and the United States appeared willing to allow aerial inspection of certain areas to prevent the secret build-up of nuclear installations. No agreement was reached, and the U.S. began photographic reconnaissance flights over Russia. In May 1960 a U.S. plane was brought down 1,200 miles inside the Soviet Union. On 5 August 1963 the U.S., Russia and Britain signed a Test Ban Treaty in Moscow, banning nuclear tests in the air, outer space and under water.

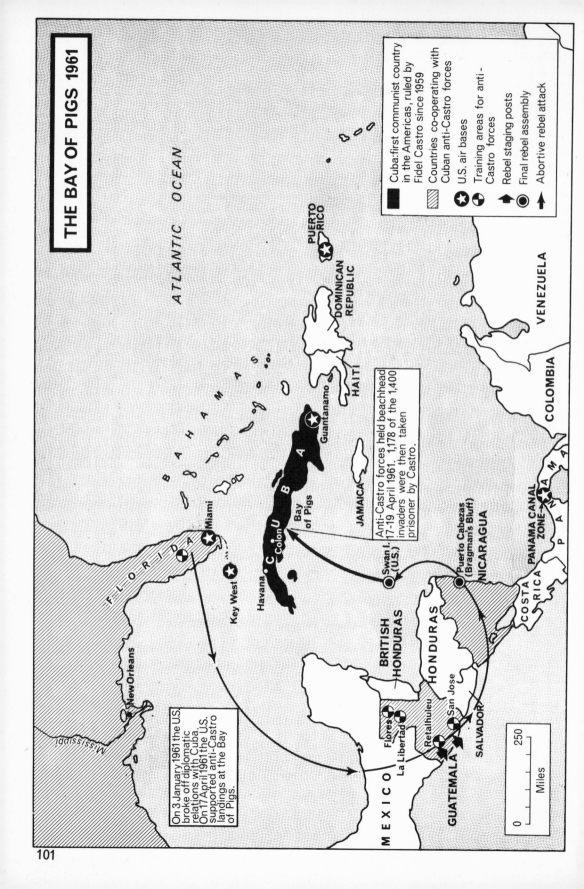

THE BAY OF PIGS 1961

ATLANTIC OCEAN

B A H A M A S

FLORIDA

Miami

Key West

New Orleans

Mississippi

C U B A

Havana

Colon

Bay of Pigs

Guantanamo

JAMAICA

HAITI

DOMINICAN REPUBLIC

PUERTO RICO

Swan I. (U.S.)

BRITISH HONDURAS

HONDURAS

MEXICO

GUATEMALA

Flores

La Libertad

Retalhuleu

San Jose

SALVADOR

Puerto Cabezas (Bragman's Bluff)

NICARAGUA

COSTA RICA

PANAMA CANAL ZONE

P A N A M A

COLOMBIA

VENEZUELA

On 3 January 1961 the U.S. broke off diplomatic relations with Cuba. On 17 April 1961 the U.S. supported anti-Castro landings at the Bay of Pigs.

Anti-Castro forces held beachhead 17-19 April 1961. 1,178 of the 1,400 invaders were then taken prisoner by Castro.

Cuba: first communist country in the Americas, ruled by Fidel Castro since 1959

Countries co-operating with Cuban anti-Castro forces

U.S. air bases

Training areas for anti-Castro forces

Rebel staging posts

Final rebel assembly

Abortive rebel attack

0   250

Miles

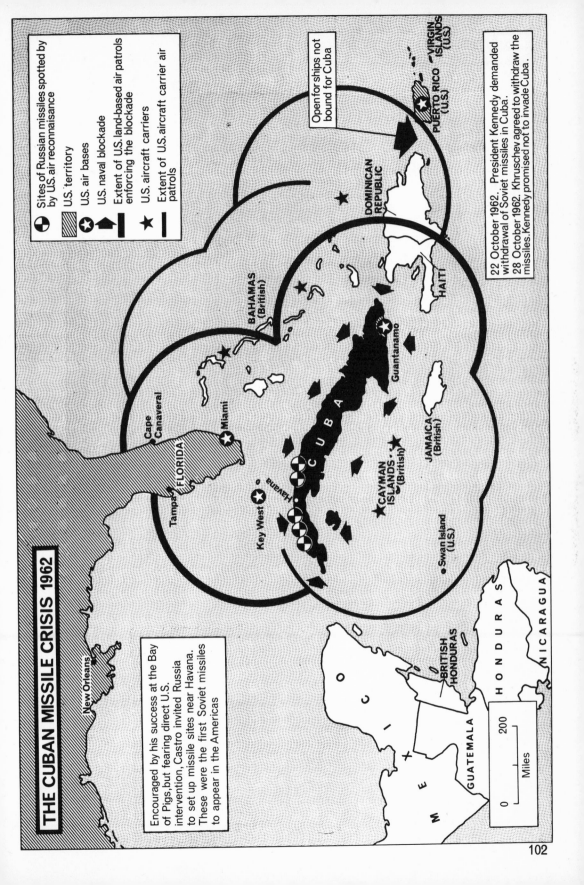

THE CUBAN MISSILE CRISIS 1962

Sites of Russian missiles spotted by U.S. air reconnaissance

U.S. territory

U.S. air bases

U.S. naval blockade

Extent of U.S. land-based air patrols enforcing the blockade

U.S. aircraft carriers

Extent of U.S. aircraft carrier air patrols

Open for ships not bound for Cuba

22 October 1962. President Kennedy demanded withdrawal of Soviet missiles in Cuba.

28 October 1962. Khruschev agreed to withdraw the missiles. Kennedy promised not to invade Cuba.

Encouraged by his success at the Bay of Pigs, but fearing direct U.S. intervention, Castro invited Russia to set up missile sites near Havana. These were the first Soviet missiles to appear in the Americas

New Orleans

FLORIDA

Cape Canaveral

Miami

Tampa

Key West

Havana

C U B A

Guantanamo

BAHAMAS (British)

Swan Island (U.S.)

CAYMAN ISLANDS (British)

JAMAICA (British)

HAITI

DOMINICAN REPUBLIC

PUERTO RICO (U.S.)

VIRGIN ISLANDS (U.S.)

M E X I C O

GUATEMALA

BRITISH HONDURAS

H O N D U R A S

NICARAGUA

0   200

Miles

102

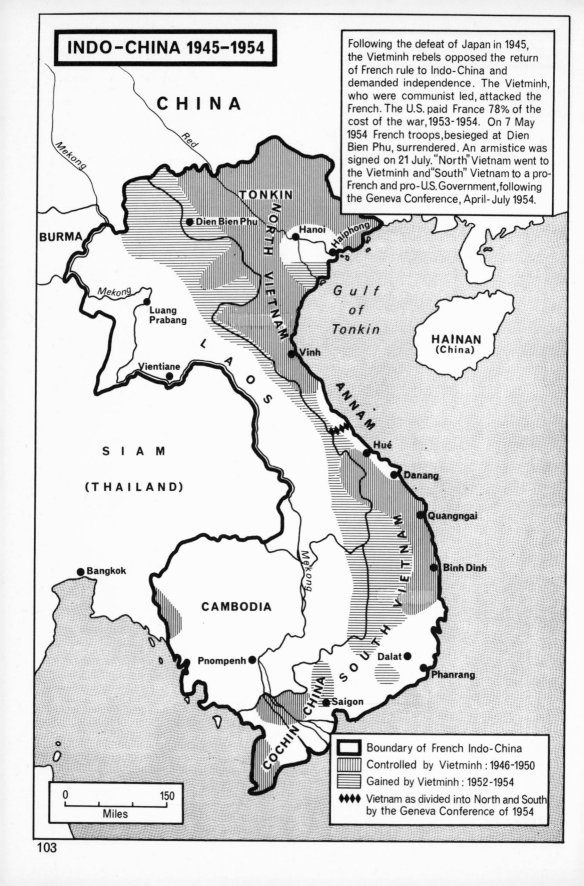

INDO-CHINA 1945–1954

Following the defeat of Japan in 1945, the Vietminh rebels opposed the return of French rule to Indo-China and demanded independence. The Vietminh, who were communist led, attacked the French. The U.S. paid France 78% of the cost of the war, 1953-1954. On 7 May 1954 French troops, besieged at Dien Bien Phu, surrendered. An armistice was signed on 21 July. "North" Vietnam went to the Vietminh and "South" Vietnam to a pro-French and pro-U.S. Government, following the Geneva Conference, April- July 1954.

CHINA

Mekong

Red

TONKIN

Dien Bien Phu

Hanoi

Haiphong

NORTH VIETNAM

BURMA

Mekong

Gulf
of
Tonkin

Luang
Prabang

HAINAN
(China)

Vientiane

Vinh

L A O S

ANNAM

Hué

S I A M

Danang

(T H A I L A N D)

Quangngai

SOUTH VIETNAM

Bangkok

Binh Dinh

Mekong

CAMBODIA

Dalat

Pnompenh

Phanrang

COCHIN CHINA

Saigon

	Boundary of French Indo-China
	Controlled by Vietminh : 1946-1950
	Gained by Vietminh : 1952-1954
◆◆◆◆	Vietnam as divided into North and South by the Geneva Conference of 1954

0   150
Miles

103

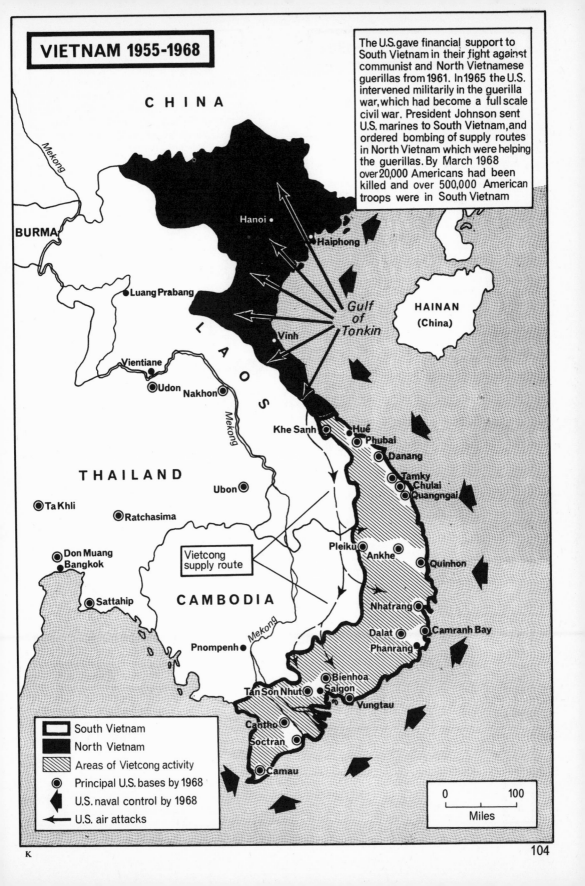

VIETNAM 1955-1968

CHINA

The U.S. gave financial support to South Vietnam in their fight against communist and North Vietnamese guerillas from 1961. In 1965 the U.S. intervened militarily in the guerilla war, which had become a full scale civil war. President Johnson sent U.S. marines to South Vietnam, and ordered bombing of supply routes in North Vietnam which were helping the guerillas. By March 1968 over 20,000 Americans had been killed and over 500,000 American troops were in South Vietnam

Mekong

BURMA

Hanoi

Haiphong

Luang Prabang

L A O S

Vinh

Gulf of Tonkin

HAINAN (China)

Vientiane

Udon Nakhon

Mekong

Khe Sanh Hué
Phubal
Danang

THAILAND

Ubon

Tamky
Chulai
Quangngai

Ta Khli

Ratchasima

Pleiku

Ankhe

Quinhon

Don Muang
Bangkok

Vietcong supply route

CAMBODIA

Nhatrang

Sattahip

Mekong

Dalat

Camranh Bay

Phanrang

Pnompenh

Bienhoa
Tan Son Nhut Saigon

Vungtau

Cantho

Soctran

Camau

	South Vietnam
	North Vietnam
	Areas of Vietcong activity
◉	Principal U.S. bases by 1968
◣	U.S. naval control by 1968
←	U.S. air attacks

0   100

Miles

K

104

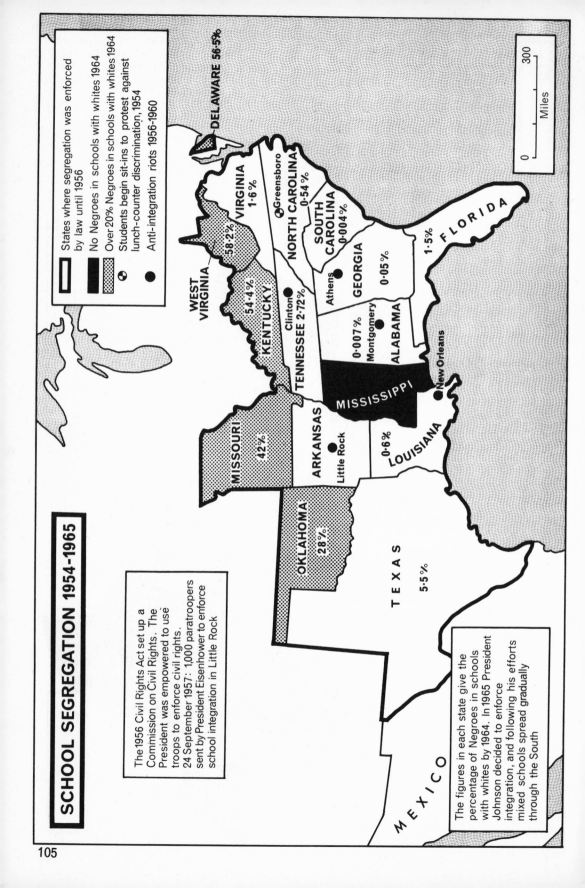

SCHOOL SEGREGATION 1954-1965

Legend:

- States where segregation was enforced by law until 1956
- No Negroes in schools with whites 1964
- Over 20% Negroes in schools with whites 1964
- Students begin sit-ins to protest against lunch-counter discrimination, 1954
- Anti-integration riots 1956-1960

The 1956 Civil Rights Act set up a Commission on Civil Rights. The President was empowered to use troops to enforce civil rights.
24 September 1957: 1,000 paratroopers sent by President Eisenhower to enforce school integration in Little Rock

The figures in each state give the percentage of Negroes in schools with whites by 1964. In 1965 President Johnson decided to enforce integration, and following his efforts mixed schools spread gradually through the South

State figures:

- DELAWARE 56·5%
- VIRGINIA 1·6%
- WEST VIRGINIA 58·2%
- NORTH CAROLINA 0·54%
- SOUTH CAROLINA 0·004%
- GEORGIA 0·05%
- FLORIDA 1·5%
- KENTUCKY 54·4%
- TENNESSEE 2·72%
- ALABAMA 0·007%
- MISSOURI 42%
- ARKANSAS
- LOUISIANA 0·6%
- OKLAHOMA 28%
- TEXAS 5·5%

Cities: Greensboro, Clinton, Athens, Montgomery, Little Rock, New Orleans

MEXICO

Miles 0 — 300

105

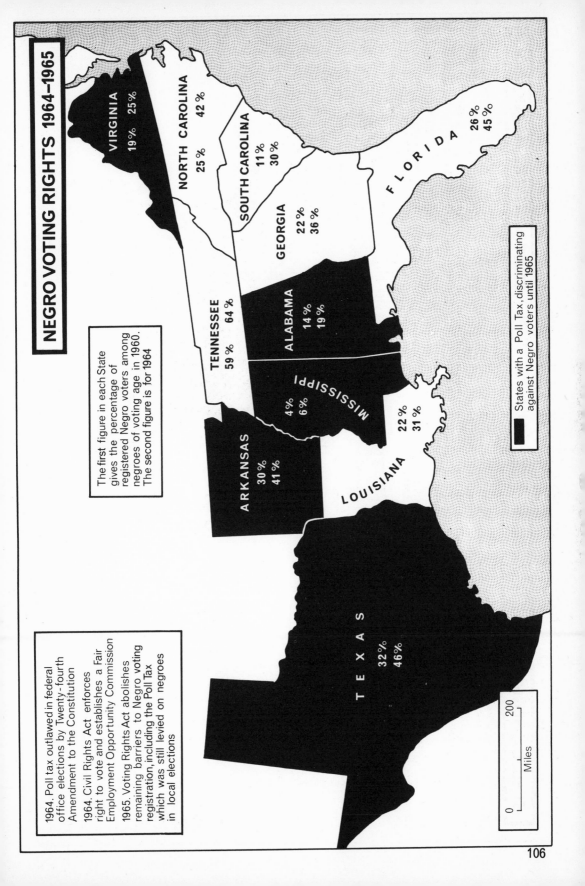

NEGRO VOTING RIGHTS 1964–1965

The first figure in each State gives the percentage of registered Negro voters among negroes of voting age in 1960. The second figure is for 1964

1964. Poll tax outlawed in federal office elections by Twenty-fourth Amendment to the Constitution

1964. Civil Rights Act enforces right to vote and establishes a Fair Employment Opportunity Commission

1965. Voting Rights Act abolishes remaining barriers to Negro voting registration, including the Poll Tax which was still levied on negroes in local elections

VIRGINIA
19 %   25 %

NORTH CAROLINA
25 %   42 %

SOUTH CAROLINA
11 %   30 %

GEORGIA
22 %   36 %

FLORIDA
26 %   45 %

TENNESSEE
59 %   64 %

ALABAMA
14 %   19 %

MISSISSIPPI
4 %   6 %

ARKANSAS
30 %   41 %

LOUISIANA
22 %   31 %

TEXAS
32 %   46 %

States with a Poll Tax, discriminating against Negro voters until 1965

0   200
Miles

106

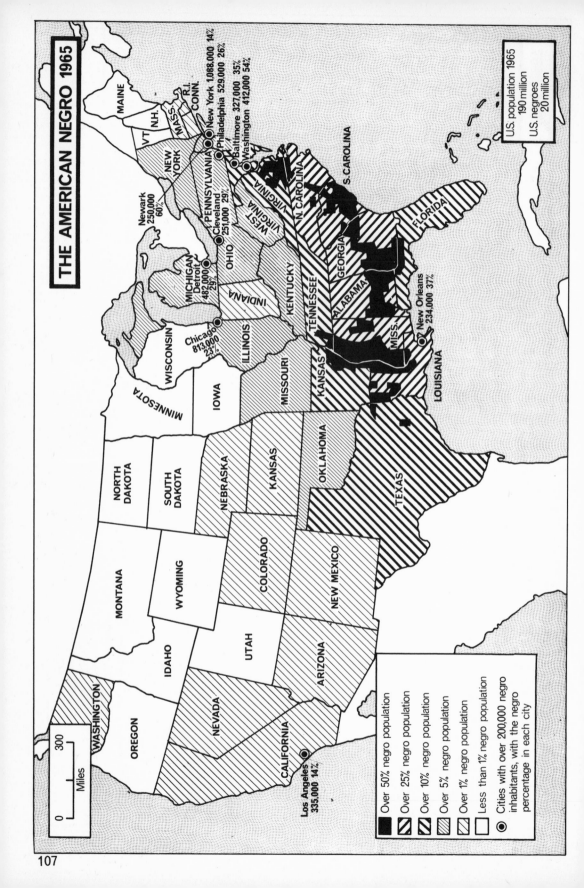

THE AMERICAN NEGRO 1965

U.S. population 1965 190 million
U.S. negroes 20 million

New York 1,088,000 14%
Philadelphia 529,000 26%
Baltimore 327,000 35%
Washington 412,000 54%
Newark 250,000 60%
Cleveland 251,000 29%
Detroit 482,000 29%
Chicago 813,000 23%
New Orleans 234,000 37%
Los Angeles 335,000 14%

MAINE
N.H.
VT
MASS.
R.I.
CONN.
NEW YORK
PENNSYLVANIA
WEST VIRGINIA
VIRGINIA
N. CAROLINA
S. CAROLINA
FLORIDA
GEORGIA
ALABAMA
TENNESSEE
KENTUCKY
MISS.
LOUISIANA
OHIO
INDIANA
MICHIGAN
ILLINOIS
WISCONSIN
MINNESOTA
IOWA
MISSOURI
ARKANSAS
OKLAHOMA
TEXAS
KANSAS
NEBRASKA
SOUTH DAKOTA
NORTH DAKOTA
COLORADO
NEW MEXICO
WYOMING
MONTANA
IDAHO
UTAH
ARIZONA
NEVADA
CALIFORNIA
OREGON
WASHINGTON

300
0
Miles

Over 50% negro population
Over 25% negro population
Over 10% negro population
Over 5% negro population
Over 1% negro population
Less than 1% negro population
Cities with over 200,000 negro inhabitants, with the negro percentage in each city

107

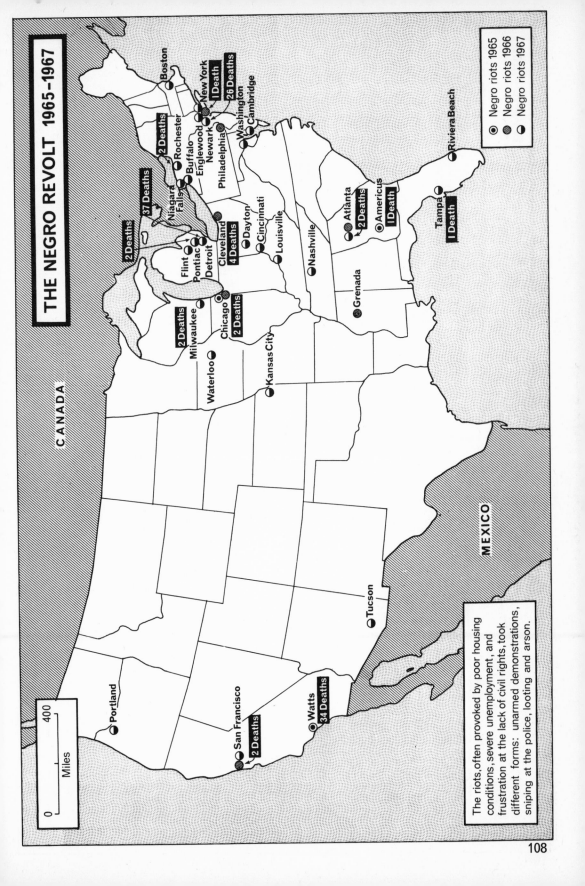

THE NEGRO REVOLT 1965-1967

CANADA

MEXICO

Negro riots 1965
Negro riots 1966
Negro riots 1967

Boston
New York — 1 Death
26 Deaths
2 Deaths — Rochester
Washington
Cambridge
Buffalo
Englewood
Newark
Philadelphia
37 Deaths — Niagara Falls
2 Deaths
Flint
Pontiac
Detroit
Cleveland — 4 Deaths
Dayton
Cincinnati
Louisville
Nashville
Atlanta — 2 Deaths
Americus — 1 Death
Tampa — 1 Death
Riviera Beach
Grenada
2 Deaths — Milwaukee
Chicago
2 Deaths
Waterloo
Kansas City
Tucson
Portland
San Francisco — 2 Deaths
Watts — 34 Deaths

0   400
Miles

The riots, often provoked by poor housing conditions, severe unemployment, and frustration at the lack of civil rights, took different forms: unarmed demonstrations, sniping at the police, looting and arson.

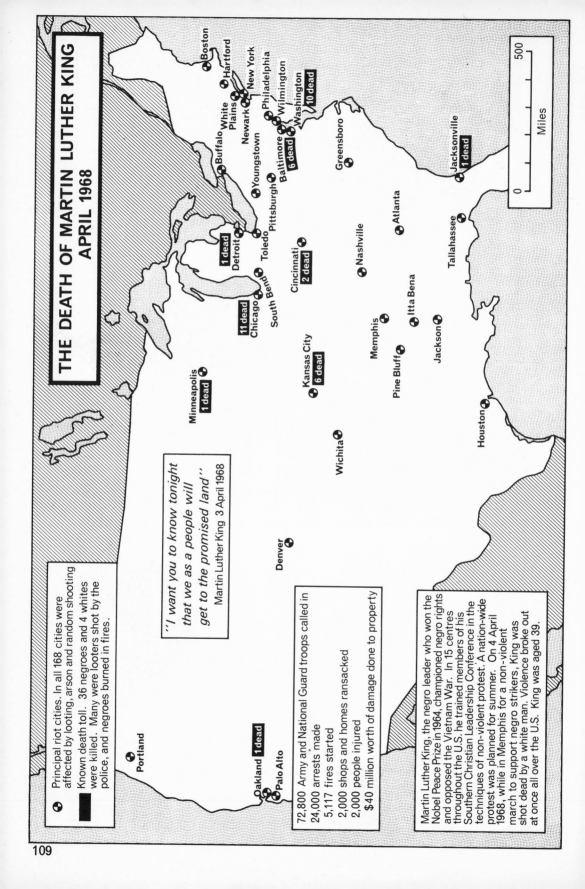

THE DEATH OF MARTIN LUTHER KING
APRIL 1968

Boston
Hartford
New York
White Plains
Buffalo
Newark
Philadelphia
Wilmington
Washington **10 dead**
Baltimore **6 dead**
Youngstown
Greensboro
Pittsburgh
Jacksonville **1 dead**
Detroit **1 dead**
Toledo
Cincinnati **2 dead**
Atlanta
Chicago **11 dead**
South Bend
Nashville
Tallahassee
Kansas City **6 dead**
Memphis
Itta Bena
Minneapolis **1 dead**
Pine Bluff
Jackson
Wichita
Houston
Denver
Portland
Oakland **1 dead**
Palo Alto

"I want you to know tonight that we as a people will get to the promised land"
Martin Luther King 3 April 1968

0   500
Miles

- Principal riot cities. In all 168 cities were affected by looting, arson and random shooting
- Known death toll. 36 negroes and 4 whites were killed. Many were looters shot by the police, and negroes burned in fires.

72,800 Army and National Guard troops called in
24,000 arrests made
5,117 fires started
2,000 shops and homes ransacked
2,000 people injured
$40 million worth of damage done to property

Martin Luther King, the negro leader who won the Nobel Peace Prize in 1964, championed negro rights and opposed the U.S. he Vietnam War. In 15 centres throughout the U.S. he trained members of his Southern Christian Leadership Conference in the techniques of non-violent protest. A nation-wide protest was planned for summer. On 4 April 1968, while in Memphis for a non-violent march to support negro strikers, King was shot dead by a white man. Violence broke out at once all over the U.S. King was aged 39.

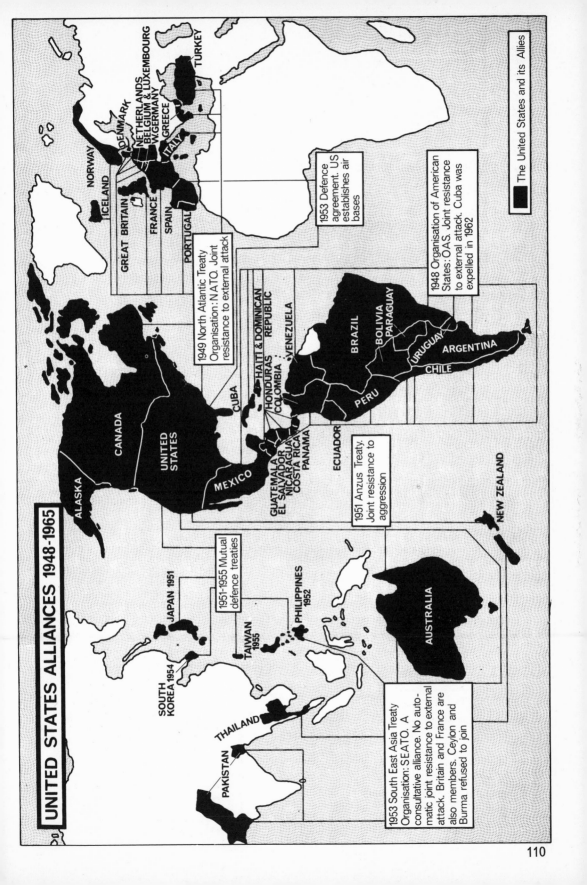

UNITED STATES ALLIANCES 1948-1965

The United States and its Allies ∎

TURKEY

NORWAY
ICELAND
DENMARK
NETHERLANDS
BELGIUM & LUXEMBOURG
W.GERMANY
GREECE
ITALY
GREAT BRITAIN
FRANCE
SPAIN
PORTUGAL

1953 Defence agreement. US establishes air bases

1949 North Atlantic Treaty Organisation: NATO. Joint resistance to external attack

1948 Organisation of American States: OAS. Joint resistance to external attack. Cuba was expelled in 1962

HAITI & DOMINICAN REPUBLIC
VENEZUELA
HONDURAS
COLOMBIA
CUBA

BRAZIL
BOLIVIA
PARAGUAY
URUGUAY
ARGENTINA
CHILE
PERU

GUATEMALA
EL SALVADOR
NICARAGUA
COSTA RICA
PANAMA
ECUADOR

MEXICO
UNITED STATES
CANADA
ALASKA

1951 Anzus Treaty. Joint resistance to aggression

NEW ZEALAND
AUSTRALIA

1951-1955 Mutual defence treaties

JAPAN 1951
SOUTH KOREA 1954
TAIWAN 1955
PHILIPPINES 1952

THAILAND
PAKISTAN

1953 South East Asia Treaty Organisation: SEATO. A consultative alliance. No automatic joint resistance to external attack. Britain and France are also members. Ceylon and Burma refused to join

110

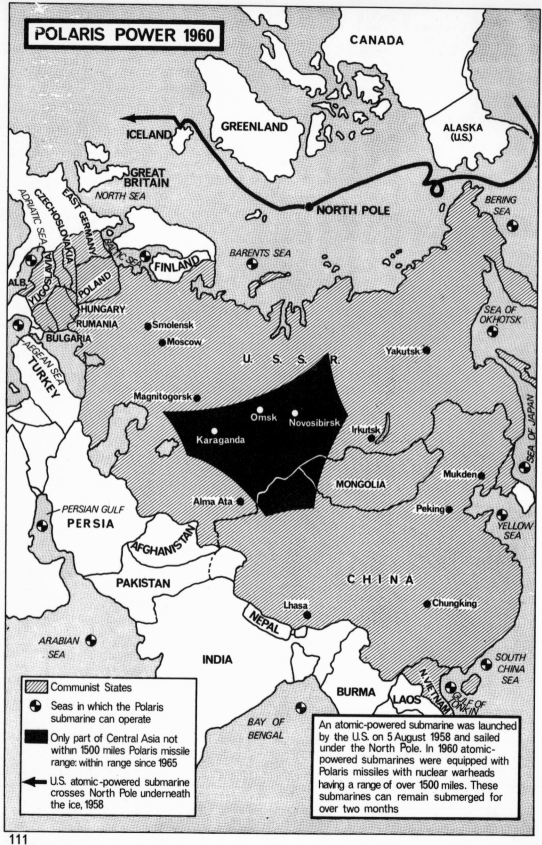

POLARIS POWER 1960

CANADA

GREENLAND

ICELAND

ALASKA (U.S.)

GREAT BRITAIN

NORTH SEA

NORTH POLE

BERING SEA

BARENTS SEA

EAST GERMANY

CZECHOSLOVAKIA

BALTIC SEA

FINLAND

ADRIATIC SEA

YUGOSLAVIA

POLAND

ALB.

HUNGARY

RUMANIA

BULGARIA

AEGEAN SEA

TURKEY

Smolensk

Moscow

U. S. S. R.

Yakutsk

SEA OF OKHOTSK

Magnitogorsk

Omsk

Novosibirsk

Irkutsk

SEA OF JAPAN

Karaganda

MONGOLIA

Mukden

PERSIAN GULF

PERSIA

Alma Ata

AFGHANISTAN

Peking

YELLOW SEA

PAKISTAN

C H I N A

Chungking

ARABIAN SEA

Lhasa

NEPAL

INDIA

BURMA

LAOS

N. VIETNAM

GULF OF TONKIN

SOUTH CHINA SEA

BAY OF BENGAL

Communist States

Seas in which the Polaris submarine can operate

Only part of Central Asia not within 1500 miles Polaris missile range: within range since 1965

U.S. atomic-powered submarine crosses North Pole underneath the ice, 1958

An atomic-powered submarine was launched by the U.S. on 5 August 1958 and sailed under the North Pole. In 1960 atomic-powered submarines were equipped with Polaris missiles with nuclear warheads having a range of over 1500 miles. These submarines can remain submerged for over two months

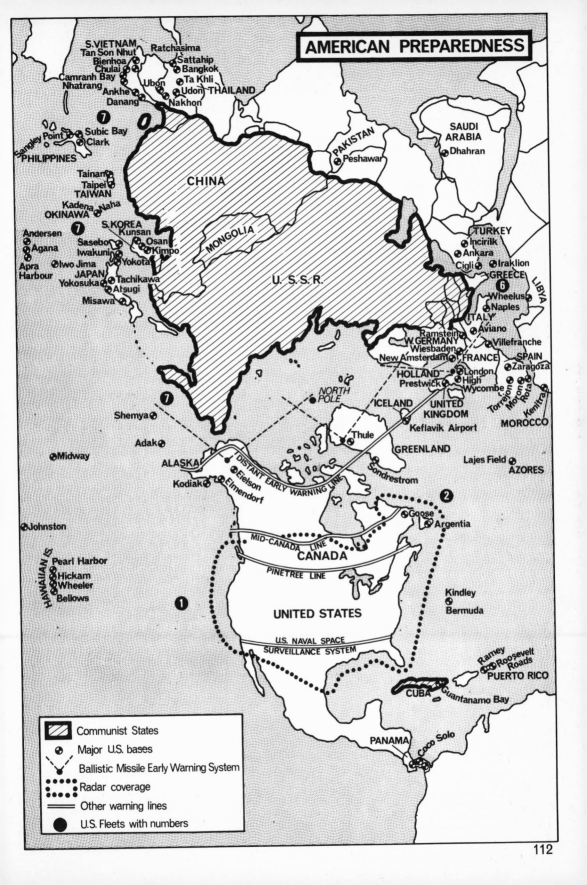

AMERICAN PREPAREDNESS

S.VIETNAM
Tan Son Nhut
Bienhoa
Chulai
Camranh Bay
Nhatrang
Ankhe
Danang

Ratchasima
Sattahip
Bangkok
Ta Khli
Ubon
Udon THAILAND
Nakhon

7

U

Sangley Point
Subic Bay
Clark
PHILIPPINES

Tainan
Taipei
TAIWAN
Kadena Naha
OKINAWA

Andersen
Agana
Apra
Harbour
Iwo Jima
JAPAN
Yokosuka
Misawa

Sasebo
Iwakuni
Yokota
Tachikawa
Atsugi

S.KOREA
Kunsan
Osan
Kimpo

7

CHINA

MONGOLIA

U.S.S.R.

PAKISTAN
Peshawar

SAUDI
ARABIA
Dhahran

TURKEY
Incirlik
Ankara
Cigli
Iraklion
GREECE
Wheelus
Naples
ITALY
Aviano
Villefranche
LIBYA

6

Ramstein
W.GERMANY
Wiesbaden
New Amsterdam
HOLLAND
Prestwick
London
High
Wycombe
UNITED
KINGDOM
Keflavik Airport
FRANCE
SPAIN
Zaragoza
Torrejon
Moron
Rota
Kenitra
MOROCCO

ICELAND

Shemya

7

Adak

Midway

Johnston

NORTH
POLE

Thule

GREENLAND

Sondrestrom

ALASKA
Kodiak
Eielson
Elmendorf

DISTANT EARLY WARNING LINE

Goose
Argentia

2

Lajes Field
AZORES

MID-CANADA LINE
CANADA
PINETREE LINE

Kindley
Bermuda

HAWAIIAN IS
Pearl Harbor
Hickam
Wheeler
Bellows

1

UNITED
STATES

U.S. NAVAL SPACE
SURVEILLANCE SYSTEM

Ramey
Roosevelt
Roads
PUERTO RICO

CUBA
Guantanamo Bay

PANAMA
Coco Solo

▨	Communist States
⊕	Major U.S. bases
⌄	Ballistic Missile Early Warning System
••••	Radar coverage
══	Other warning lines
●	U.S. Fleets with numbers